The Deceitful Calm
Edmund Blunden

THE SKYLARK

A singing firework, the sun's darling, —
Hark how ~~the an anget~~ creation pleads!

Then silence: ~~and~~ see,
~~Is quickly turned~~ a small gray bird
That runs among the weeds.

LARK DESCENDING

A singing firework, the sun's darling, —
Hark how creation pleads!
Then silence: see, a small gray bird
That runs among the weeds.

THE DECEITFUL CALM

Poems by
EDMUND BLUNDEN
A NEW SELECTION

EDITED BY
RENNIE PARKER & MARGI BLUNDEN

LAUREL BOOKS

First published in 2006
by Laurel Books
282 The Common Holt Wiltshire BA14 6QJ

Printed by Antony Rowe Ltd
Bumpers Farm Chippenham Wiltshire SN14 6LH

Poems by Edmund Blunden in this volume are reproduced by
arrangement with the Estate of Mrs Claire Blunden

Introduction © Rennie Parker, 2006
Preface and Notes © Margi Blunden, 2006

The rights of
Rennie Parker as author of the introduction and of
Margi Blunden as author of the preface and notes to this work
are asserted in accordance with
Section 77 of the Copyright, Designs and Patents Act 1988

British Library Cataloguing in Publication Data
A CIP record for this book is available from the British Library

ISBN 1-873390-08-4

Cover photograph reproduced by arrangement with the Estate of
Mrs Claire Blunden

Cover designed by Jane Stephenson

CONTENTS

NOTES

GOUZEAUCOURT: THE DECEITFUL CALM

How unpurposed, how inconsequential
Seemed those southern lines when in the pallor
    Of the dying winter
    First we went there!

Grass thin-waving in the wind approached them,
Red roofs in the near view feigned survival,
    Lovely mockers, when we
    There took over.

There war's holiday seemed, nor though at known times
Gusts of flame and jingling steel descended
    On the bare tracks, would you
    Picture death there.

Snow or rime-frost made a solemn silence,
Bluish darkness wrapped in dangerous safety;
    Old hands thought of tidy
    Living-trenches!

There it was, my dears, that I departed,
Scarce a greater traitor ever! There too
    Many of you soon paid for
    That false mildness.

PREFACE

Some years ago I inherited several boxes containing many decades of my father's and mother's assorted papers. Exploring them, my interest in my father's work grew and it was a fortuitous day when I met Rennie Parker as we found we both had the desire to present Blunden to a new readership. The final result of that initial meeting is this book, and I am delighted to introduce it to whoever has a curiosity about a man who strode his own path in the pages of literature, at a time when other poets were making reputations for breaking links with the past, both in style and subject matter in the modernist trend.

Blunden always held true to his individual voice, which was shaped by his rural upbringing, Christ's Hospital School, the First World War, the Far East and his interest in literature, especially of the 18th and 19th centuries.

The integrity of Blunden the writer was a reflection of the man. It was this integrity which was acutely tested during the Great War and afterwards. That he suffered from post traumatic stress is now clear, but when I was a child the expression of his anger and depression were not fully understood.

The difference for him from many other soldiers was that his creative ability helped him to maintain his sanity, whilst others, having survived, then killed themselves in despair. If as a youngster I witnessed a man suffering from the effects of a kind of torture that very few of us alive today have experienced, I also knew a man who had the capacity to love and be loved in an extraordinary way.

He had an enormous belief in the value and capability of the individual and one of the hallmarks of his personality was his encouragement of others. Combined with his love of cricket, nature, books and literature, this brought him friendships and respect across the globe.

Poetically he had a response to the world which enabled him to see beyond the particular detail to its wide context. He seldom judged a situation in terms of how it presented itself, as his concern was to understand what lay behind the appearance, thus offering the reader something to think about for themselves. When he was asked a question his answers may often have seemed indirect, but he was simply directing the questioner to find his or her own answer.

Blunden loved humanity, and was unafraid to point out its complex nature in his poetry. Whilst he has been criticised for being impersonal, his intention is to present *poetic* truths and this meant keeping himself in the background. The result of this is that as a poet he achieves "intellectual and imaginative poise" (John Johnston, *English Poetry of the First World War,* Princeton University Press, 1964). He also achieves emotional poise and these three qualities allow the reader the freedom to muse for themselves on the issues he presents.

If we assume Blunden to be a conservative poet we are deceived. What he does is to disturb the apparent. Glancing at often unnoticed details of life in his calm, structured format, he then changes things by turning the perceived situation on its head. We are at once given something larger and more important than previously supposed. He was interested in the eternal laws of the universe and their relationship to mankind and poetry was for him the medium to reflect on these. He is not simply a war poet or a nature poet but a poet of human nature who renounces every label and category and asks that we look a little more closely at 'things quiet and unconcerned' in our universe.

In this book we have attempted to present something a little different and have been guided by Blunden's own annotations, some of which are included in the end notes. Finally my thanks to Martin Chown, my husband, for his unfailing encouragement and patience in the making of this selection.

Margi Blunden

October 2005

INTRODUCTION

The titles and contents of my books *The Waggoner* and *The Shepherd* have, I apprehend, done me a slight injustice; that is, they have labelled me among the poets of the time as a useful rustic, or perhaps not so useful — one of the class whom the song describes:

> I sits with my feet in a brook;
> If anyone asks me for why,
> I hits him a whack with my crook —
> "It's Sentiment kills me," says I.

So complained Edmund Blunden, poet, critic, scholar, and literary all-rounder, in the Preface to his mid-career *Poems 1914-1930* (Cobden-Sanderson, 1930). Earlier, aghast at the continued popularity of his 18th century-based "Almswomen," he couldn't help saying "Why should all my poems be neglected in order that 'Almswomen' may abound?" (Webb, p.115). He was labelled as a sentimental Georgian whether he liked it or not, and as other poets from the same generation discovered, such labels proved hard to live down.

Yet village life in 1916 still bore more resemblance to the world of Thomas Gray and William Collins than anything we might observe now. Haycocks and hop poles stood up as Blunden describes, and his childhood was spent in a village where he observed at first hand the rural characters and Hardyesque domestic tragedies which later informed his poetry. The pond described in "The Midnight Skaters" was a real one at Yalding in Kent, and his almswomen were two elderly friends who lived at Kirtling, near Newmarket. It was not idealism which prompted his mature verse, but a love of the countryside and a respect for its people and traditions.

It was only after 1918 that pre-war poetic sensitivities towards rural idealism became unfashionable. This was partly due to a second wave of Georgian poets whose works were forgettable by any standards, unlike the strongly felt poems of Edward Thomas and the unsettling twilight world of Walter de la Mare. Blunden's late and somewhat unfortunate timing meant that he nearly missed the Georgian anthologies altogether, appearing only in the final volume of Eddie Marsh's series in 1922 when the movement was under attack from urbanite modernists.

Eddie Marsh — arts patron, editor, and secretary to Sir Winston Churchill — had never heard of Blunden at all until *Harbingers* appeared on his desk in September 1919, along with a note explaining that Siegfried Sassoon had prompted him to send it along. Marsh was soon convinced that he was dealing with a genuine poet, and he forwarded Blunden some of his patronage money, aware that the young man was probably badly off and in need of encouragement. This injection of establishment support was exactly what Blunden needed, and before long he was at work on the poems which made his reputation. His second full collection *The Shepherd*, published in April 1922, won him much critical acclaim and the prestigious Hawthornden Award, catapulting him into the front line of literary London.

Character sketches would often describe him as "birdlike" and modest amid the literary heavyweights of the period, yet his overall shy temperament did not exclude ambition and determination. For all his love of books, he survived two years in the trenches (he was the longest-serving war poet) and he was awarded the Military Cross — a feat which he decided to omit from his autobiography of those years.

Initially, Blunden's work bridged the gap between old and new styles, traditional in concept yet informed by precise imagery and a unique double vision as a result of his war-haunted imagination. His talent as a classicist at Christ's Hospital had already provided him with fluent versemaking abilities, and his earliest published works show his complete confidence with rhyme schemes despite the study-room feel to his stanzas. It is important to realise from the start that Blunden uses archaism and pastoralism for specific ends, particularly where war is the main subject matter. Usually, his pastoral imagery is a way of distancing himself from the horror of the Western Front while at the same time pointing out the contrast between what "is" and what "was." Later on, it emphasises his dislocation from the postwar world, where he is viewing the new fields of a revised England with an ironic mindset based on bitter experience.

This ability to set up and then undermine the pastoral ideal is one of Blunden's great hallmarks as a poet, one which can be found in many poems included in this selection. In "The Baker's Van," a somewhat cosy image of a rural tradesman is soon replaced by the knowledge that his life is one of stunted frustration — he was a schoolboy with talent, one who could have risen above his circumstances. He observes the young Blunden about to take the road which he was denied, and the last line leaves us in no doubt that he lives with a sense of unfulfilled longing: "still in a brown study seen." Elsewhere, Blunden portrays the underlying violence of country life ("The Giant Puffball") and he seems unsure of whether the natural world is on our side or not: in "The Kiss" he begins "I am for the woods against the world/But are the woods for me?" He was never entirely sure. Like Robert Frost, he had "a perception of unyielding nature, that repels man's attempts at communion or description" (Marsack, p.23).

There were other Georgians who could tackle these aspects of magic and moonlight and the darker side of nature. But Blunden's fear seems altogether more psychological, no matter how often it is dressed up in neatly presented verses. We can see where this tendency came from — it was not only an inbuilt sense of otherness and prescience, because he was prone to visionary episodes, although his biographer provides few details on this.[1] It was the experience of the First World War, which left him permanently at odds with the world, impressing on his mind just at the point when he became a professional poet. He sees what is apparent on the surface, and then the grinning skull beneath the skin.

Like Robert Graves, he passed straight from the world of public school and into the theatre of war, with little time to adjust to adulthood. As described in the 1990 biography by Barry Webb, Blunden felt that he was never fully present in the real world thereafter:

Since 1918 hardly a day or night passed without my losing the present and living in a ghost story. Even when the detail of dreams is fantasy, the setting of that strange world insists on torturing.

This appeared in the *Daily Express* as late as 1968, showing the effects of what contemporary psychologists would describe as post traumatic stress disorder. And sometimes, this unreality and dislocation was written directly into the poetry. In "The Lost Battalion," Blunden's unit patrols a nameless and featureless No Man's Land with a sense of rising panic, aware that they will reach their destination all the same. It is the world of a recurring nightmare, one of the many which Blunden experienced throughout his life as a result of serving his country. Yet living out this nightmare would give him a deep empathy towards poets whose own lives were clouded with madness and misunderstanding. By 1920, he had embarked on rescuing John Clare from obscurity, and later on, he would be the first successful editor of Ivor Gurney.

Blunden was always praised for his polished craftsmanship and his abilities within formal constraints. "Vlamertinghe, Passing the Chateau, July 1917" is a brief example of how much he could achieve within his boundaries. What appears as a simple poem — flowers for the men, and a reference to redness as blood — is built on layers of poetry and history which a poet motivated purely by the war might find unnecessary for the purpose.

It is one of his best known poems, with its prose equivalent appearing in *Undertones of War,* where the origins of several other poems can be found. Blunden describes the abundance of a chateau garden and contrasts it with the surrounding circumstances; a familiar enough device. But he starts by quoting from Keats' "Ode to a Grecian Urn," a stanza beginning "Who are these coming to the sacrifice?"

"And all her silken flanks with garlands drest" —
But we are coming to the sacrifice.

In Keats' poem, the object dressed with flowers is a cow about to be sacrificed, while the carved figures on the Grecian urn will never grow old. It is a scene frozen in time, divorced from contemporary reality. Keats' poem also includes the significant line "When old age shall this generation waste," surely prompting a combination of ideas which Blunden had in mind — there in front of him was a generation about to be wasted, enjoying a moment of peace as they passed the chateau. Keats' line implies that time will be ageing the onlookers and wasting them away, but to Blunden and his later readers, it recalls the old men at HQ ensuring the destruction of youth.

It is necessary to read Keats' poem before realising this added dimension to Blunden's work, because it is an unexpectedly academic poem. This is also reflected in the form, which is a variation on a Petrarchan sonnet, complete with a turn of emphasis in the last six lines. Traditionally, this form is used for sequences and love poetry, exactly the opposite to the type of subject matter he is using. As in other poems, Blunden takes a literary convention and turns it on its head. In one short poem, he demonstrates both his dependence on literary culture, his originality in using old forms for new purposes, and finally his contemporary influence coming from trench humour and colloquialism in the last two lines. He is not concerned with the remote world of classical reference, but with what happens when people die horribly in the present, when form and perfection are broken.

Some startling and rewarding features of Blunden's style are found in "Third Ypres," a difficult narrative poem which needs some explanation here for first time readers. It owes its origins to a traumatic period where two of the central events — that of the signaller being shot and the doctor being killed in the pillbox — happened close to him within the same twenty four hours (Webb, p.77). Both incidents were written into his diary, and he was probably using the prose account when he drafted the poem. It is a rare example of Blunden unleashing his dramatic potential, and it is worth studying alongside Owen's work.

"Third Ypres" opens on a scene of rejoicing as the men in their trenches realise that they have survived another attack. They wonder why things are so quiet — it transpires that most of their companions, who were moving forward for an attack, are dead in the trenches beyond. The weather deteriorates and tensions mount, with the soldiers' worst fears hanging unspoken in the air around them: "they've all died on the entanglements."

14

Then Blunden snaps out of his linear narrative and writes a visionary episode, covering three versions of the recent past. A signaller has died; Blunden passes him first while he was alive and carrying out his duties:

> You I passed by this emplacement
> You whom I warned, poor daredevil, waving your flags

And then again when the signaller is recently dead:

> Among this screeching I pass you again and shudder
> At the lean green flies upon the red flesh madding

and thirdly, he has the misfortune to see again the moment of death — Blunden (revisiting the scene in his imagination) pulls the signaller over to receive a message before he transforms like a figure in a dream.

In these few lines, Blunden plays with parallel timescales, a device which naturally interests him as a man who lived with too many literary ghosts; the shade of John Clare visits him in 'Clare's Ghost', one of the few surviving poems which he wrote in the trenches. But in 'Third Ypres', time is stretched out as well as doubled back on itself. "Sure as a runner time himself's accosted" he writes, "And the slow moments shake their heavy heads." Tension and fear have produced the familiar phenomenon of hours crawling along at an unbearable pace while the waiting men sit and stew. Meanwhile, the silence is so tense that a creaking chair becomes a significant noise.

After the parallel signaller episode, he snaps back into life in the trenches (another shift in perspective — he is now "back then" as a participating linear narrator) and the company spends a night waiting for their next orders. They are due to relieve the forward trench companions whom they cannot contact — at this point, suspecting their deaths. But it ends in tragedy; while Blunden's company moves into the forward trench, they suffer a massive enemy bombardment, and he is trapped in a concrete pillbox with three other men. You suspect that the three others are killed — the Doctor certainly is, as we see from Blunden's frantic attempts to revive him. Just when he is about to get help from his newly arrived sergeant, the sergeant has even worse news for him. Their headquarters have received a direct hit, forty men have been killed, and the sergeant is the only survivor. Blunden realises that his own experience has been overtaken by a greater horror, and the poem ends on a question, with the situation in deadlock:

> But who with what command can now relieve
> The dead men from that chaos, or my soul?

The postwar Blunden never found an answer to this dilemma.

The poem is both epic and dramatic, with passages reminiscent of an important Shakespearian speech where the hero is faced with insurmountable odds. Blunden's cadences in blank verse lines such as "the mind swoons doubly burdened" and "Where still the brain devises some last armour/To live out the poor limbs," would sound equally good on the stage in 1597. But the doctor episode is noticeable for its overtones of Marlowe too, recalling the climactic scene where Dr. Faustus is about to be dragged off to Hell. While Marlowe's Faustus dies at daybreak, aware that the sun is rising: "See where Christ's blood streams in the firmament," Blunden is trying to drag his innocent doctor out of the pillbox — out of the threatening hell — and into the "pure and sacred day." It is worth examining the original Marlovian lines for the echoes which Blunden is writing. In addition, Blunden invests his own literary rhetoric with absolute precision; he does not let his apostrophising spin out of control. His "sepulchre" is literary and appropriate to the deathly subject matter, but it is also a vault-like concrete or stone structure, not much different from the shape of his World War pillbox.

Apart from the Elizabethan influence, Blunden uses archaic word inversions for a specific reason, usually to point out something false or ironic. "Here stood we...," "So shouting dug we..." he writes, near the beginning of the poem. He could easily use the modern word order, because it would not affect the metre of the line. What it does affect is how the event is perceived. The soldiers believe they have won at this point — they have survived another night and they are not yet aware of why their sector is ominously quiet. They have false optimism, expressed in a mock heroic tone; they are trampling down the enemy, but it might as well be yesterday's newspapers for all the good it does. They are unaware of what lies in store for them, although Blunden the poet with hindsight can pile on the dramatic irony. He uses the same technique a little later on: "Comes there no word," he begins pompously, only to be contradicted by the fear that no words and no people will be coming. He uses archaism to set something up, only to knock it down with brutality and realism.

Blunden the ruralist makes an appearance too — both in terms of description and in finding a vehicle for a much deeper metaphor. For example, see his image of the barbed wire, standing up "like an unplashed hedge and thorned with giant spikes." The thorny wire is bushy and uncontrolled, equipped with surreal oversized barbs, not compact and well-tended like its green equivalent. When he mentions the men who have died on the wire, its woodiness and thorns help to give the scene religious overtones, with its associations of the holy cross and the crown of thorns. Blunden's soldiers would have been Sussex countrymen, real-life hedge layers and craftsmen, all images of God's creation who were now being crucified on the giant hedge from hell.

It is not too far-fetched to imagine this religious dimension. Popular verse and propagandist writings often depicted the soldier as Christ-like, and it is hard to imagine Blunden being unaware of them. Later, while editing Wilfred Owen's manuscripts in 1931, he was much impressed by the statement: "Christ is literally in No Man's Land. There men often hear His voice." (Webb, p.93). But in "Third Ypres" Blunden's originality surfaces where he places religious imagery into the landscape and not so much into the soldiers, as propagandists would do. For Blunden (not a traditionally religious man) God and religion could always be expressed through the natural world and the art of poetry, an affinity he shared with the Romantics.

His narrative style is admirably suited to the relating of confused real life experiences; he can shift from one event to another and change gear between literary and colloquial modes without sounding inconsistent. His furnace of differing reactions and emotions help to make it a deep and interesting poem — he is active, yet he is impotent in the circumstances; he is overwhelmed, yet he is able to recall incidents; he hates the effects of war, and yet he still upholds its rules. These contradictions are modern in the way they change quickly and jostle side by side, and Blunden's versatility may come as a surprise to readers who have only seen a few short poems in anthologies. This important poem, unfashionably long but as powerful as anything by Owen, is also discussed by Desmond Graham and Martin Taylor in their assessments of his work.

Blunden may have identified with his rural upbringing, yet the reality of his life after 1918 was very different. He was an Oxford scholar and a published writer; and he soon found that the first few literary jobs which came his way were insufficient for a married man with young children. In June 1918 he had married Mary Daines, an attractive dark-haired Suffolk girl — but this impulsive act meant that the university withdrew his scholarship money, and the Blundens stared poverty in the face. By 1924 he had no option except to take a lecturing post offered by the Imperial University in Tokyo, embarking on a career which would keep him overseas for the next three years.

Luckily for Blunden, his tenure of the post had followed the disastrous lectureship of Robert Nichols, an erratic man who found the Japanese puzzling and alien, resenting their culture instead of working within it, as Blunden would do. Where Nichols had failed, Blunden would succeed. He came to love and respect the Far East, and collections such as *A Japanese Garland* (1928) and *A Hong Kong House* (1962) record his encounters with its people and landscapes. His continued contribution as a long-term cultural ambassador resulted in his election to the Japan Academy in 1950, a very rare honour for a Westerner. Through him, a generation of academics developed a love of British literature.

Despite the new start and the regular income provided by the Tokyo post, Mary had decided to stay in England with their two children, and the marriage did not survive. In 1933 he married Sylva Norman, an Armenian writer from Manchester who collaborated with him on a novel, *We'll Shift Our Ground,* published the same year. She appears to have been a complicated and highly strung person; her literary interests and sensitivity were not enough to prevent the relationship from running aground long before 1945. He was rescued at last by Claire Poynting, a student from St. Hilda's who attended his lectures at Merton College, Oxford, where he had taught as a Fellow since 1931. This third marriage endured, and Claire willingly packed her suitcase when the Blundens were posted to Hong Kong in 1953.

The essential paradox of Blunden's career is that a poet so committed to England and Englishness should find himself working abroad for so many years — and these absences from the UK poetry scene did nothing for his artistic reputation between the wars. It was easy to regard him as unfashionable and literally off the map. A similar fate befell Robert Graves, who had emigrated to Mallorca in 1929, and the South African-born satirist Roy Campbell, who set up home in Spain. In Blunden's case, he was not helped by the vast distances and Japan's involvement in the Second World War.

His prolific writing was another stumbling block, for a reader can spot the same themes reappearing in slightly different disguises over a number of collections. It is safe to say that he had fallen into the trap of writing too much within a relatively narrow range of themes, even though this situation was forced on him by the need to make a realistic income. The problem is not that his styles remained the same, but that his talent matured early and the reading public had already encountered his expert command of form and cadence, associating it with an older period of literature.

His work-rate is surprising even now. By the age of forty four he had produced more than ten poetry collections as well as major editions of Clare, Smart, Collins, Keats and Shelley, Charles Lamb, and Wilfred Owen. He had written the first biography of Leigh Hunt, translated Henry Vaughan's Latin poems, and provided two versions of his own experience, *De Bello Germanico* and *Undertones of War*. Still to come were Hardy, a popular life of Shelley, and more editions of the Romantic poets; by the end of his career, his books would also include collections of essays, lectures, and celebrations of English life and institutions. *Cricket County* (1944) was a reflection of his love for the game, something which he shared with his lifelong friend, Siegfried Sassoon.

He was also far from being a dry, over-serious writer. A number of poems (some included here) supply his amused reactions and wry observations, while his private book dedications and letters — all written in his exemplary pattern-book handwriting — recall surreal dialogues and daft asides which could only be made by one who was animated and humorous by nature despite what the war had done to him. Comedy and tragedy could be found side by side, for example in the poem "Country Sale," where the sad belongings of a bankrupt householder are presided over by a "jumped-up jerky cockerel on his box."

Blunden was a loyal friend too, staying in contact with regimental colleagues. He accumulated people easily, and he found it hard to say no when students and writers demanded his attention. Always ready for a challenge, he assisted the composer Gerald Finzi during the latter's lengthy campaign to get Gurney's work into print, something finally achieved through Hutchinson in 1954. But it was not without its problems, since the Blundens were packing for abroad again, and Finzi virtually kept him under house arrest until the work was completed.

The introduction to Blunden's selection, reprinted in a later Chatto & Windus edition of 1973, is a good example of him as a critic; all the more remarkable for it having been written at one sitting. It is sympathetic and attentive to detail, combining a slightly old fashioned, polite sensibility with poetic, acute phrasing which helps to bring the subject alive:

> His [Gurney's] poetry has its sweetness but it has sharpness
> and severity, or what he calls 'patterns like earth-sense
> strong' — something of the high-poised gargoyle against the
> flying cloud....neither pussy-cat sentiment nor an indifferent

'eye on the object' can be imputed to him, nor yet trivial languor nor studied homeliness of expression.

Readers soon suspect that any dead poets revisited by Edmund Blunden would be justly presented and well supported.

Students of Shelley may also find his 1946 biography worth having. Despite being written during wartime and without access to the special collections available to later scholars, it is nevertheless packed with quotations and a great read, still an informative and lively introduction to the poet. His association with Gerald Finzi would bear other fruit too. Several of the composer's best known songs are Blunden settings, with two appearing in the song cycle *Oh Fair To See*.[2]

Blunden knew that his own poetry was out of fashion, but he kept his integrity and wrote about the subjects he knew best, independently of the movements happening during the century. He may have guessed that the pendulum would swing again; while for him, poetry itself was always one of the universal truths:

> When one has read poetry for so long as I, too, have, a preface like this may be expected to include a word on the old question, what it is. [....] I have seen with surprise how beloved examples have abruptly become horrible examples, and how a new day blows its trumpets for writings hard to connect with what *was* poetry just before. The principal thing is still with me; poetry is as much a part of the universe as mathematics and physics.
>
> (Preface, *Poems of Many Years*, Collins, 1957).

After two years as Professor of Poetry at Oxford (1966-1968), Blunden retired again to Long Melford in Suffolk, the county he had known best after Kent and Sussex. He is buried in the graveyard of Holy Trinity church, under a stone inscribed 'I live still/to love still/things quiet/& unconcerned', a reflection of the modesty which was so noticeable to his contemporaries during his lifetime.

Rennie Parker   October 2005

NOTES

1. As a small child, EB heard distant gunfire from France, a sound identical to that heard later on the Western Front; while looking out of his bedroom window, he saw an unusual cloud formation which he later recognised as the buildings of Christ's Hospital (mentioned by Webb). Both premonitions heralded life-changing incidents which no-one could possibly imagine at the time. Trench life brought him into contact with 'otherness' too — once, he saw an evening-suited man who vanished into thin air before him.

2. For details about EB's work with Gerald Finzi, see Stephen Banfield, *Gerald Finzi: An English Composer* (Faber, 1997).

FURTHER READING

Edmund Blunden: A Biography Barry Webb (Yale, 1990)

Edmund Blunden: Overtones of War: Poems of the First World War, ed. Martin Taylor (Duckworth, 1996)

Edmund Blunden: Poetry and Prose ed. Kenneth Hopkins (Rupert Hart-Davis, 1950)

Edmund Blunden: Selected Poems ed. Robyn Marsack, (Carcanet, 1982, 1993)

The Truth of War: Owen, Blunden, and Rosenberg Desmond Graham (Carcanet 1984)

A Hong Kong House: Poems 1951-1961 Edmund Blunden (Collins, 1962)

Poems,1914-1930 Edmund Blunden (Cobden-Sanderson, 1930)

Poems,1930-1940 Edmund Blunden (Macmillan, 1940)

Poems of Many Years Edmund Blunden (Collins, 1957)

Undertones of War Edmund Blunden (Collins, 1964; also Penguin Modern Classics, 1982)

CHRONOLOGY

1 Nov. 1896 Edmund Charles Blunden born in London, to schoolteacher parents. He is the first in a family of nine.

1900 Move to Yalding in Kent.

1909 Wins a scholarship to Christ's Hospital, Horsham.

1914 Senior Classics Scholarship, Queen's College, Oxford.

May 1916 In France with the 11th Royal Sussex; posted to Festubert, Cuinchy, Richebourg, the Somme.

13 Nov. 1916 Awarded the Military Cross.

1917 Ypres, then Passchendaele.

1 June 1918 Marries Mary Daines; two daughters (Joy and Clare), one son (John).

June 1920 Begins work for *The Athenaeum*.

Nov. 1920 *The Waggoner*.

April 1922 *The Shepherd*. Wins the Hawthornden Award.

March 1924 Leaves England for Imperial University, Tokyo.

July 1927 Back in England, working for *The Nation*.

Nov. 1928 *Undertones of War*— a beststeller.

Feb. 1931 Divorce granted; Mary remarries.

March 1931 Merton College, Oxford. Fellow and Tutor in English. *The Poems of Wilfred Owen*.

5 July 1933 Marries writer Sylva Norman.

1942 Resigns from Merton after his second marriage ends. Joins the *Times Literary Supplement*.

29 May 1945 Marries Claire Poynting; four daughters, Margaret, Lucy, Frances, Catherine.

6 Nov. 1947 In Japan as Cultural Liaison Officer for the British Mission.

May 1950 Returns to England and works again for the *TLS*.

Sept. 1953 Professor of English Hong Kong University.

1954 Editions of Ivor Gurney and Percy Bysshe Shelley.

1956 Queen's Gold Medal for Poetry.

1966 Succeeds Robert Graves as Professor of Poetry at Oxford.

1968 Resigns his Oxford Professorship on medical advice and retires to Long Melford in Suffolk.

20 Jan. 1974 Dies at Hall Mill, Long Melford, aged 77.

BEGINNINGS

THE PREAMBLE

I sing of the loves I have had, of the
  folk and the times and the places
That look to have left me for ever: but
  still they have left their traces
Deep in my heart; if you are a lover of sorrow
  or joy,
Listen, and learn the delights that have
  passioned the heart of a boy.

I sing of the rivers and hamlets and woodlands
  of Sussex and Kent,
Such as I know them: I found a delight wherever I went,
By plat and by hatch, through acres of hops or
  of corn.
I sing of the friends I have made, and the one
  or two who would mourn.

BY CHANCTONBURY

We shuddered on the blotched and
    wrinkled down,
So gaunt and chilled with solitary
    breeze.
Sharp stubborn grass, black heather-trails, wild
    trees
Knotting their knared wood like a thorny
    crown —
Huge funnelled dips to chalklands straked with
    brown
White railway smoke-drifts dimming by degrees,
Slow ploughs afield, flood waters on the leas,
And red roofs of the small, ungainly town:
And blue fog over all, and saddening all —
Thus lay the landscape. Up from the sea there
    loomed
A stately airship, clear and large awhile:
Then, gliding grandly inland many a mile,
It left our Druid height that black groves
    plumed,
Vanishing fog-like in the foggy pall.

THE BARN *(final four stanzas)*

The barn is old, and very old,
But not a place of spectral fear.
Cobwebs and dust and speckling sun
Come to old buildings every one.
Long since they made their dwelling here,
      And here you may behold

Nothing but simple wane and change;
Your tread will wake no ghost, your voice
Will fall on silence undeterred.
No phantom wailing will be heard,
Only the farm's blithe cheerful noise;
      The barn is old, not strange.

The superstition dies away,
And through the minds of country men
A callous thought of life has passed,
And myth and legend-lore are cast
Far from the modern yeoman's ken,
      Fears of a bygone day.

Something is lost, perhaps: the old
Simplicity of rustic wit
Is banished by the rude disdain
And pride that speaks a boorish brain,
The pride that kills the fear of it,
      And strikes its kindness cold.

ALMSWOMEN

At Quincey's moat the squandering village ends,
And there in the almshouse dwell the dearest friends
Of all the village, two old dames that cling
As close as any trueloves in the spring.
Long, long ago they passed threescore-and-ten,
And in this doll's house lived together then;
All things they have in common, being so poor,
And their one fear, Death's shadow at the door.
Each sundown makes them mournful, each sunrise
Brings back the brightness in their failing eyes.

How happy go the rich fair-weather days
When on the roadside folk stare in amaze
At such a honeycomb of fruit and flowers
As mellows round their threshold; what long hours
They gloat upon their steepling hollyhocks,
Bee's balsams, feathery southernwood, and stocks,
Fiery dragon's-mouths, great mallow leaves
For salves, and lemon-plants in bushy sheaves,
Shagged Esau's-hands with five green finger-tips.
Such old sweet names are ever on their lips.
As pleased as little children where these grow
In cobbled pattens and worn gowns they go,
Proud of their wisdom when on gooseberry shoots
They stuck eggshells to fright from coming fruits
The brisk-billed rascals; pausing still to see
Their neighbour owls saunter from tree to tree,
Or in the hushing half-light mouse the lane
Long-winged and lordly.
                              But when those hours wane,
Indoors they ponder, scared by the harsh storm
Whose pelting saracens on the window swarm,
And listen for the mail to clatter past

And church clock's deep bay withering on the blast;
They feed the fire that flings a freakish light
On pictured kings and queens grotesquely bright,
Platters and pitchers, faded calendars
And graceful hour-glass trim with lavenders.

Many a time they kiss and cry, and pray
That both be summoned in the selfsame day,
And wiseman linnet tinkling in his cage
End too with them the friendship of old age,
And all together leave their treasured room
Some bell-like evening when the may's in bloom.

MAN AND NATURE

MALEFACTORS

Nailed to these green laths long ago,
You cramp and shrivel into dross,
Blotched with mildews, gnawed with moss,
And now the eye can scarcely know
The snake among you from the kite —
　　　So sharp does Death's fang bite.

I guess your stories; you were shot
Hovering above the miller's chicks;
And you, coiled on his threshold bricks —
Hissing, you died; and you, Sir Stoat,
Dazzled with stable man's lantern stood
　　　And tasted crabtree wood.

Here then, you leered-at luckless churls,
Clutched to your clumsy gibbet shrink
To shapeless orts; hard by the brink
Of this black scowling pond that swirls
To turn the wheel beneath the mill,
　　　The wheel so long since still.

There's your revenge, the wheel at tether,
The miller gone, the white planks rotten,
The very name of the mill forgotten,
Dimness and silence met together...
Felons of fur and feather, can
　　　There lurk some crime in man –

In man, your executioner,
Whom here Fate's cudgel battered down?
Did he too filch from squire and clown?...
The damp dust makes the ivy whir
Like passing death, the sluices well,
　　　Dreary as a passing-bell.

29

NOVEMBER MORNING

From the night storm sad wakes the winter day
With sobbings round the yew, and far-off surge
Of broadcast rain; the old house cries dismay,
And rising floods gleam silver on the verge
Of sackclothed skies and melancholy grounds.
On the black hop-pole beats the weazen bine,
The rooks with terror's tumult take their rounds,
Under the eaves the chattering sparrows pine.

Waked by the bald light from his bed of straw,
The beggar shudders out to steal and gnaw
Sheep's locusts: leaves the last of many homes —
Where mouldered apples and black shoddy lie,
Hop-shovels spluttered, wickered flasks flung by,
And sharded pots and rusted curry-combs.

MOLE CATCHER

With coat like any mole's, as soft and black
And hazel bows bundled beneath his arm,
And long-helved spade and rush bag on his back,
The trapper plods alone about the farm:
And spies new mounds in the ripe pasture-land,
And where the lob-worms writhe up in alarm
And easy sinks the spade, he takes his stand
Knowing the moles' dark highroad runs below:
Then sharp and square he chops the turf, and day
Gloats on the opened turnpike through the clay.

Out from his wallet hurry pin and prong,
And trap, and noose to tie it to the bow;
And then his grand arcanum, oily and strong,
Found out by his forefather years go
To scent the peg and witch the moles along.
The bow is earthed and arched ready to shoot
And snatch the death-knot fast round the first mole
Who comes and snuffs well pleased and tries to root
Past the sly nose peg; back again is put
The mould, and death left smirking in the hole.
The old man goes and tallies all his snares
And finds the prisoners there and takes his toll.

And moles to him are only moles; but hares
See him afield and scarcely cease to nip
Their dinners, for he harms not them; he spares
The drowning fly that of his ale would sip
And throws the ant the crumbs of comradeship.
And every time he comes into his yard
Grey linnet knows he brings the groundsel sheaf,
And clatters round the cage to be unbarred,
And on his finger whistles twice as hard. —
What his old vicar says, is his belief,
In the side pew he sits and hears the truth;
And never misses once to ring his bell
On Sundays night and morn, nor once since youth
Has heard the chimes afield, but has heard tell
There's not a peal in England sounds so well.

DEATH OF CHILDHOOD BELIEFS

There the puddled lonely lane,
    Lost among the red swamp sallows,
Gleams through drifts of summer rain
    Down to ford the sandy shallows,
Where the dewberry brambles crane.

And the stream in cloven clay
    Round the bridging sheep-gate stutters,
Wind-spun leaves burn silver-grey,
    Far and wide the blue moth flutters
Over swathes of warm new hay.

Scrambling boys with mad to-do
    Paddle in the sedges' hem,
Ever finding joy anew;
    Clocks toll time out — not for them,
With what years to frolic through!

How shall I return and how
    Look once more on those old places!
For Time's cloud is on me now
    That each day, each hour effaces
Visions once on every bough.

Stones could talk together then,
    Jewels lay for hoes to find,
Each oak hid King Charles agen,
    Ay, nations in his powdered rind;
Sorcery lived with homeless men.

Spider Dick, with cat's green eyes
    That could pierce stone walls, has flitted —
By some hedge he shakes and cries,
    A lost man, half-starved, half-witted,
Whom the very stoats despise.

Trees on hill-tops then were Palms,
    Closing pilgrims' arbours in;
David walked there singing Psalms;
    Out of the clouds white seraphin
Leaned to watch us fill our bin.

Where's the woodman now to tell
    Will o' the Wisp's odd fiery anger?
Where's the ghost to toll the bell
    Startling midnight with its clangour
Till the wind seemed but a knell?

Drummers jumping from the tombs
    Banged and thumped all through the town,
Past shut shops and silent rooms
    While the flaming spires fell down; —
Now but dreary thunder booms.

Smuggler trapped in headlong spate,
    Smuggler's mare with choking whinney,
Well I knew your fame, your fate;
    By the ford and shaking spinney
Where you perished I would wait,

Half in glory, half in fear,
    While the fierce flood, trough and crest,
Whirled away the shepherd's gear,
    And sunset wildfire coursed the west,
Crying Armageddon near.

THE GIANT PUFFBALL

From what proud star I know not, but I found
    Myself newborn below the coppice rail,
No bigger than the dewdrops and as round,
    In a soft sward, no cattle might assail.

And here I gathered mightiness and grew
    With this one dream kindling in me: that I
Should never cease from conquering light and dew
    Till my white splendour touched the trembling sky.

A century of blue and stilly light
    Bowed down before me, the dew came agen,
The moon my sibyl worshipped through the night,
    The sun returned and long revered: but then

Hoarse drooping darkness hung me with a shroud
    And switched at me with shrivelled leaves in scorn:
Red morning stole beneath a grinning cloud,
    And suddenly clambering over dike and thorn

A half-moon host of churls with flags and sticks
    Hallooed and hurtled up the partridge brood,
And Death clapped hands from all the echoing thicks,
    And trampling envy spied me where I stood;

Who haled me tired and quaking, hid me by,
    And came agen after an age of cold,
And hung me in the prison-house a-dry
    From the great crossbeam. Here defiled and old

I perish through unnumbered hours, I swoon,
    Hacked with harsh knives to staunch a child's torn hand;
And all my hopes must with my body soon
    Be but as crouching dust and wind-blown sand.

COUNTRY SALE

Under the thin green sky, the twilight day,
The old home lies in public sad array,
Its time being come, the lots ranged out in rows,
And to each lot a ghost. The gathering grows
With every minute, neckcloths and gold pins;
Poverty's purples; red necks, horny skins,
Odd peeping eyes, thin lips and hooking chins.

Then for the skirmish, and the thrusting groups
Bidding for tubs and wire and chicken coops,
While yet the women hang apart and eye
Their friends and foes and reckon who will buy.
The noisy field scarce knows itself, not one
Takes notice of the old man's wavering moan
Who hobbles with his hand still brushing tears
And cries how this belonged here sixty years,
And picks his brother's picture from the mass
Of frames; and still from heap to heap folks pass.

The strife of tongues even tries the auctioneer,
Who, next the dealer smirking to his leer,
A jumped-up jerky cockerel on his box,
Runs all his rigs, cracks all his jokes and mocks;
"Madam, now never weary of well-doing",
The heavy faces gleam to hear him crowing.
And swift the old home's fading. Here he bawls
The white four-poster, with its proud recalls,
But we on such old-fashioned lumber frown;
"Passing away at a florin", grins the clown.
Here Baskett's Prayer Book with his black and red
Finds no more smile of welcome than the bed,
Though policeman turn the page with wisdom's looks:
The hen-wives see no sense in such old books.
Here painted trees and well-feigned towers arise
And ships before the wind, that sixpence buys.

All's sold; then hasty vanmen pile and rope
Their loads, and ponies stumble up the slope.
And all are gone, the trampled paddock's bare;
The children round the buildings run and blare,
Thinking what times these are! not knowing how
The heavy-handed fate has brought them low,
Till quartern loaf be gone too soon today,
And none is due tomorrow. Long, then, play,
And make the lofts re-echo through the eve,
And sweeten so the bitter taking-leave.

So runs the world away. Years hence shall find
The mother weeping to her lonely mind,
In some new place, thin set with makeshift gear,
For the home she had before the fatal year;
And still to this same anguish she'll recur,
Reckoning up her fine old furniture,
The tall clock with his church-bell time of day,
The mirror where so deep the image lay,
The china with its rivets numbered all,
Seeming to have them in her hands — poor soul,
Trembling and crying how these, loved so long,
So beautiful, all went for an old song.

WINTER: EAST ANGLIA

In a frosty sunset
  So fiery red with cold
The footballers' onset
  Rings out glad and bold;
Then boys from daily tether
  With famous dogs at heel
In starlight meet together
  And to farther hedges steal;
Where the rats are pattering
  In and out the stacks,
Owls with hatred chattering
  Swoop at the terriers' backs.
And, frost forgot, the chase grows hot
  Till a rat's a foolish prize,
But the cornered weasel stands his ground,
Shrieks at the dogs and boys set round,
Shrieks as he knows they stand all round
  And hard as winter dies.

THE MIDNIGHT SKATERS

The hop-poles stand in cones,
  The icy pond lurks under,
The pole-tops steeple to the thrones
  Of stars, sound gulfs of wonder;
But not the tallest there, 'tis said,
Could fathom to this pond's black bed.

Then is not death at watch
  Within those secret waters?
What wants he but to catch
  Earth's heedless sons and daughters?
With but a crystal parapet
Between, he has his engines set.

Then on, blood shouts, on, on,
  Twirl, wheel and whip above him,
Dance on this ball-floor thin and wan,
  Use him as though you love him;
Court him, elude him, reel and pass,
And let him hate you through the glass.

A TRANSCRIPTION

"This young man comes from your way, Tom."
                    At this
The old thin silent fellow on the sack,
Who turned some pages with a face of lead,
Clapt eyes on me. His quivering jaw released
Words sere and rambling as November leaves.
"You come from my way...Ah, I used to know
Sturmere, New England, Stoke, the Valley Arms.
'Tis forty years ago. 'Tis changed, no doubt.
Yes, I knew all them places."
                          Here the master
Of the old-clothes shop pointed me again,
"He went a-cricketin' out to Stoke Whit-Monday.
"Cricketin'? Ah, there warn't no cricket then,
Except the boys might take a bat at nights.
The men ne'er played no cricket nor no quoits
Nor football. Tenpins — that was all there was."
And pausing, he gave ear to something afar
And suddenly heard what made his words ring out.
"But we had music in the churches then,
The clar'net on a Sunday used to play
In Sturmere church — and as the sayen is,
The clar'net used to sound like heaven on earth."
O Love, your anthem reached the dealer's den,
The rags and rubbish thence all-glorious shone.
And he again: "There's no such music now,
There's nothen now for nobody, only sorrow."

THE BAKER'S VAN

Village children shouted shrill,
"What ch'er, Baker!" "Way up, Will!"
As I passed he stopped his van
To tell me, "Your luck's in, old man.

"I was nothing but a fool
When left your father's school;
He said many and many a time
If I wanted, I could climb.

"He said, he'd not had one more quick
At history and arithmetic,
He framed my drawings for the wall,
An oak leaf and a cricket ball.

"But my dad, you know, was stiff,
And laughed and huffed — There's always's If;
There's none of us been scholars yet,
There's honest work for us to get.

"So here I am; and there are you,
Always starting something new;
They tell me, if you shine this way,
It's college for you some fine day.

"Good boy!" He sighed; and called his horse,
And drove upon his daily course,
And when he called at Golden Green
Was still in a brown study seen.

THE MATCH

In a round cavern of glass, in steely water
(None yet so comfortless appalled the day)
A man-eel poised, his lacquer-skin disparted
In desert reds and wharfy green; his eyes too
Burned like beads of venom.
Beyond the glass the torturer stood, with thrustings,
Passes, grimaces, toothy grins, warped oeillades.
To this black magic mania's eel retorted
With fierce yet futile muzzle, and lancing darted
In an electric rapine, against the wall
Of glass, or life: those disputants of nothing
So acidly attracting, lovingly loathing,
Driven by cold radii, goblin lovers, seemed yet
The difficult dumb-show of my generation.

WAR AND ITS AFTERMATH

FESTUBERT : THE OLD GERMAN LINE

Sparse mists of moonlight hurt our eyes
With gouged and scourged uncertainties
Of soul and soil in agonies.

One derelict grim skeleton
That drench and dry had battened on
Still seemed to wish us malison;

Still zipped across the gouts of lead
Or cracked like whipcracks overhead;
The gray rags fluttered on the dead.

THIEPVAL WOOD

The tired air groans as the heavies swing over, the river-hollows
      boom;
The shell-fountains leap from the swamps, and with wildfire and
      fume
The shoulder of the chalkdown convulses.
Then the jabbering echoes stampede in the slatting wood,
Ember-black the gibbet trees like bones or thorns protrude
From the poisonous smoke – past all impulses.
To them these silvery dews can never again be dear,
Nor the blue javelin-flame of thunderous noons strike fear.

BLEUE MAISON

Now to attune my dull soul, if I can,
To the contentment of this countryside
Where man is not forever killing man
But quiet days like these calm waters glide.
And I will praise the blue flax in the rye,
And pathway bindweed's trumpet-like attire,
Pink rest-harrow and curlock's glistening eye,
And poppies flaring like St. Elmo's fire.

And I will praise the willows silver-gray,
And where I stand the road is rippled over
With airy dreams of blossomed bean and clover,
And shyest birds come elfin-like to play:
And in the rifts of blue above the trees
Pass the full sails of natural Odysseys.

CLARE'S GHOST

Pitch-dark night shuts in, and the rising gale
  Is full of the presage of rain,
  And there comes a withered wail
  From the wainscot and jarring pane,
  And a long funeral surge
  Like a wood god's dirge,
Like the wash of the shoreward tides, from the firs on the crest.

The shaking hedges blacken, the last gold flag
  Lowers from the west;
The Advent bell moans wild like a witch hag
  In the storm's unrest,
And the lychgate lantern's candle weaves a shroud,
  And the unlatched gate shrieks loud.

Up fly the smithy sparks, but are baffled from soaring
  By the pelting scurry, and ever
As puff the bellows, a multitude more outpouring
  Die foiled in the endeavour;

And a stranger stands with me here in the glow
Chinked through the door, and marks
    The sparks
Perish in whirlpool wind, and if I go
To the delta of cypress, where the glebe gate cries,
I see him there, with his streaming hair
    And his eyes
Piercing beyond our human firmament,
Lit with a burning deathless discontent.

REUNION IN WAR

The windmill in his smock of white
    Stared from his little crest,
Like a slow smoke was the moonlight
    As I went like one possessed

Where the glebe path makes shortest way;
    The stammering wicket swung.
I passed amid the crosses grey
    Where opiate yew-boughs hung.

The bleached grass shuddered into sighs,
    The dogs that knew this moon
Far up were harrying sheep, the cries
    Of hunting owls went on.

And I among the dead made haste
    And over flat vault stones
Set in the path unheeding paced
    Nor thought of those chill bones.

Thus to my sweetheart's cottage I,
    Who long had been away,
Turned as the traveller turns adry
    To brooks to moist his clay.

Her cottage stood like a dream, so clear
    And yet so dark; and now
I thought to find my more than dear
    And if she'd kept her vow.

Old house-dog from his barrel came
    Without a voice, and knew
And licked my hand; all seemed the same
    To the moonlight and the dew.

By the white damson then I took
    The tallest osier wand

And thrice upon her casement strook,
    And she, so fair, so fond,

Looked out, and saw in wild delight,
    And tiptoed down to me,
And cried in silent joy that night
    Beside the bullace tree.

O cruel time to take away,
    Or worse to bring agen;
Why slept not I in Flanders clay
    With all the murdered men?

For I had changed, or she had changed,
    Though true loves both had been,
Even while we kissed we stood estranged
    With the ghosts of war between.

We had not met but a moment ere
    War baffled joy, and cried,
"Love's but a madness, a burnt flare;
    The shell's a madman's bride."

The cottage stood, poor stone and wood,
    Poorer than stone stood I;
Then from her kind arms moved in a mood
    As grey as the cereclothed sky.

The roosts were stirred, each little bird
    Called fearfully out for day;
The church clock with his dead voice whirred
    As if he bade me stay

To trace with foolish fingers all
    The letters on the stones
Where thick beneath the twitch roots crawl
    In dead men's envied bones.

1916 SEEN FROM 1921

Tired with dull grief, grown old before my day,
I sit in solitude and only hear
Long silent laughters, murmurings of dismay,
The lost intensities of hope and fear;
In those old marshes yet the rifles lie,
On the thin breastwork flutter the grey rags,
The very books I read are there — and I
Dead as the men I loved, wait while life drags

Its wounded length from those sad streets of war
Into green places here, that were my own;
But now what once was mine is mine no more,
I seek such neighbours here and I find none.
With such strong gentleness and tireless will
Those ruined houses seared themselves in me,
Passionate I look for their dumb story still,
And the charred stub outspeaks the living tree.

I rise up at the singing of a bird
And scarcely knowing slink along the lane,
I dare not give a soul a look or word
For all have homes and none's at home in vain:
Deep red the rose burned in the grim redoubt,
The self-sown wheat around was like a flood,
In the hot path the lizards lolled time out,
The saints in broken shrines were bright as blood.

Sweet Mary's shrine between the sycamores!
There we would go, my friend of friends and I,
And snatch long moments from the grudging wars,
Whose dark made light intense to see them by.
Shrewd bit the morning fog, the whining shots
Spun from the wrangling wire; then in warm swoon
The sun hushed all but the cool orchard plots,
We crept in the tall grass and slept till noon.

A FARM NEAR ZILLEBEKE

Black clouds hide the moon, the amazement is gone;
The morning will come in weeping and rain;
The Line is all hushed — on a sudden anon
The fool bullets clack and guns mouth again.
I stood in the yard of a house that must die,
And still the black hame was stacked by the door,
And harness still hung there, and the dray waited by.

Black clouds hid the moon, tears blinded me more.

BEHIND THE LINE

Treasure not so the forlorn days
When dun clouds flooded the naked plains
   With foul remorseless rains;
   Tread not those memory ways
Where by the dripping alien farms,
Starved orchards with their shrivelled arms,
The bitter mouldering wind would whine
At the brisk mules clattering towards the Line.

Remember not with so sharp skill
Each chasm in the clouds that with strange fire
   Lit pyramid-fosse and spire
   Miles on miles from our hill;
In the magic glass, aye, then their lure
Like heaven's houses gleaming pure
Might soothe the long-imprisoned sight
And put the double storm to flight.

Enact not you so like a wheel
The round of evenings in sandbagged rooms
   Where candles flicked the glooms;
   The jests old time could steal
From ugly destiny, on whose brink
The poor fools grappled fear with drink,
And snubbed the hungry raving guns
With endless tunes on gramophones.

About you spreads the world anew,
The old fields all for your sense rejoice,
   Music has found her ancient voice,
   From the hills there's heaven on earth to view;
And kindly Mirth will raise his glass
With you to bid dull Care go pass —
And still you wander muttering on
Over the shades of shadows gone.

THIRD YPRES, A REMINISCENCE

Triumph! how strange, how strong had triumph dawned
On weary hate of foul and endless war,
When from its grey gravecloths awoke anew
The summer day. Among the tumbled wreck
Of fascined lines and mounds the light was peering,
Half-smiling upon us, and our new-found pride; —
The terror of the waiting night outlived;
The time too crowded for the heart to count
All the sharp cost in friends killed on the assault.
No sap of all the octopus had held us,
Here stood we trampling down the ancient tyrant.
So shouting dug we among the monstrous pits.

Amazing quiet fell upon the waste,
Quiet intolerable, to those who felt
The hurrying batteries beyond the masking hills
For their new parley setting themselves in array
In crafty fourms unmapped.
                              No, these, smiled faith,
Are dumb for the reason of their overthrow.
They move not back, they lie among the crews,
Twisted and choked, they'll never speak again.
Only the copse where once might stand a shrine
Still clacked and suddenly hissed its bullets by.

The War would end, the Line was on the move,
And at a bound the impassable was passed.
We lay and waited with extravagant joy.

Now dulls the day and chills; comes there no word
From those who swept through our new lines to flood
The lines beyond? but little comes, and so
Sure as a runner time himself's accosted.
And the slow moments shake their heavy heads,
And croak, "They're done, they'll none of them get through,"
They're done, they've all died on the entanglements,

The wire stood up like an unplashed hedge, and thorned
With giant spikes — and there they've paid the bill.

Then comes the black assurance, then the sky's
Mute misery lapses into trickling rain,
That wreathes and swims and soon shuts in our world.
And those distorted guns, that lay past use,
Why — miracles not over! — all a-firing,
The rain's no cloak from their sharp eyes. And you,
Poor signaller, you I passed by this emplacement,
You whom I warned, poor dare-devil, waving your flags,
Among this screeching I pass you again and shudder
At the lean green flies upon the red flesh madding.
Runner, stand by a second. Your message.— He's gone,
Falls on a knee, and his right hand uplifted
Claws his last message from his ghostly enemy,
Turns stone-like. Well, I liked him, that young runner,
But there's no time for that. O now for the word
To order us flash from these drowning roaring traps
And even hurl upon that snarling wire?
Why are our guns so impotent?
                              The grey rain,
Steady as the sand in an hourglass on this day,
Where through the window the red lilac looks
And all's so still, the chair's odd click is noise, —
The rain is all heaven's answer, and with hearts
Past reckoning we are carried into night,
And even sleep is nodding here and there.

The second night steals through the shrouding rain,
We in our numb thought crouching long have lost
The mockery triumph, and in every runner
Have urged the mind's eye see the triumph to come,
The sweet relief, the straggling out of hell
Into whatever burrows may be given
For life's recall. Then the fierce destiny speaks.
This was the calm, we shall look back for this.
The hour is come; come, move to the relief!

Dizzy we pass the mule-strewn track where once
The ploughman whistled as he loosed his team;
And where he turned home-hungry on the road
The leaning pollard marks us hungrier turning.
We crawl to save the remnant who have torn
Back from the tentacled wire, those whom no shell
Has charred into black carcasses — Relief!
They grate their teeth until we take their room,
And through the churn of moonless night and mud
And flaming burst and sour gas we are huddled
Into the ditches where they bawl sense awake
And in a frenzy that none could reason calm
(Whimpering some, and calling on the dead)
They turn away; as in a dream they find
Strength in their feet to bear back that strange whim
Their body.

    At the noon of the dreadful day
Our trench and death's is on a sudden stormed
With huge and shattering salvoes, the clay dances
In founts of clods around the concrete sties
Where still the brain devises some last armour
To live out the poor limbs.
      This wrath's oncoming
Found four of us together in a pillbox,
Skirting the abyss of madness with light phrases,
White and blinking, in false smiles grimacing.
The demon grins to see the game, a moment
Passes, and — still that drum-tap dongs my brain
To a whirring void — through the great breach above me
The light comes in with icy shock and the rain
Horridly drips. Doctor, talk, talk! If dead
Or stunned I know not; the stinking powdered concrete,
The lyddite turns me sick — my hair's all full
Of this smashed concrete. O I'll drag you, friends,
Out of the sepulchre into the light of day:
For this is day, the pure and sacred day.
And while I squeak and gibber over you,

Out of the wreck a score of field-mice nimble,
And tame and curious look about them. (These
Calmed me, on these depended my salvation.)

There comes my sergeant, and by all the powers
The wire is holding to the right battalion
And I can speak — but I myself first spoken
Hear a known voice now measured even to madness
Call me by name: "For God's sake send and help us,
Here in a gunpit, all headquarters done for,
Forty or more, the nine-inch came right through.
All splashed with arms and legs, and I myself
The only one not killed, not even wounded.
You'll send — God bless you." The more monstrous fate
Shadows our own, the mind droops doubly burdened,
Nay all for miles our anguish groans and bleeds,
A whole sweet countryside amuck with murder,
Each moment puffed into a year with death.

Still wept the rain, roared guns,
Still swooped into the swamps of flesh and blood
All to the drabness of uncreation sunk,
And all thought dwindled to a moan, — Relieve!
But who with what command can now relieve
The dead men from that chaos, or my soul?

RURAL ECONOMY (1917)

There was winter in those woods,
    And still it was July:
There were Thule solitudes
    With thousands huddling nigh;
There the fox had left his den,
The scraped holes hid not stoats but men.

To these woods the rumour teemed
    Of peace five miles away;
In sight, hills hovered, houses gleamed
    Where last perhaps we lay
Till the cockerels bawled bright morning and
The hours of life slipped the slack hand.

In sight, life's farms sent forth their gear;
    Here rakes and ploughs lay still;
Yet, save some curious clods, all here
    Was raked and ploughed with a will.
The sower was the ploughman too,
And iron seeds broadcast he threw.

What husbandry could outdo this?
    With flesh and blood he fed
The planted iron that nought amiss
    Grew thick and swift and red,
And in a night though ne'er so cold
Those acres bristled a hundredfold.

Why, even the wood as well as field
    This ruseful farmer knew
Could be reduced to plough and tilled,
    And if he'd planned, he'd do;
The field and wood, all bone-fed loam,
Shot up a roaring harvest-home.

TWO VOICES

"There's something in the air," he said
   In the large parlour cool and bare;
The plain words in his hearers bred
   A tumult, yet in silence there
All waited; wryly gay, he left the phrase,
Ordered the march and bade us go our ways.

"We're going South, man"; as he spoke
   The howitzer with huge ping-bang
Racked the light hut; as thus he broke
   The death-news, bright the skylarks sang;
He took his riding-crop and humming went
Among the apple-trees all bloom and scent.

Now far withdraws the roaring night
   Which wrecked our flower after the first
Of those two voices; misty light
   Shrouds Thiepval Wood and all its worst:
But still "There's something in the air" I hear,
And still "We're going South, man," deadly near.

THE ZONNEBEKE ROAD

Morning, if this late withered light can claim
Some kindred with that merry flame
Which the young day was wont to fling through space!
Agony stares from each gray face.
And yet the day is come; stand down! stand down!
Your hands unclasp from rifles while you can,
The frost has pierced them to the bended bone?
Why, see old Stevens there, that iron man,
Melting the ice to shave his grotesque chin:
Go ask him, shall we win?
I never liked this bay, some foolish fear
Caught me the first time that I came in here;
That dugout fallen in awakes, perhaps,
Some formless haunting of some corpse's chaps.
True, and wherever we have held the line,
There were such corners, seeming-saturnine
For no good cause.
                Now where Haymarket starts,
That is no place for soldiers with weak hearts;
The minenwerfers have it to the inch.
Look, how the snow-dust whisks along the road,
Piteous and silly; the stones themselves must flinch
In this east wind; the low sky like a load
Hangs over — a dead-weight. But what a pain
Must gnaw where its clay cheek
Crushes the shell-chopped trees that fang the plain —
The ice-bound throat gulps out a gargoyle shriek.
The wretched wire before the village line
Rattles like rusty brambles or dead bine,
And then the daylight oozes into dun;
Black pillars, those are trees where roadways run.
Even Ypres now would warm our souls; fond fool,
Our tour's but one night old, seven more to cool!
O screaming dumbness, O dull clashing death,
Shreds of dead grass and willows, homes and men,
Watch as you will, men clench their chattering teeth
And freeze you back with that one hope, disdain.

PILLBOX

Just see what's happening, Worley! — Worley rose
And round the angled doorway thrust his nose
And Sergeant Hoad went too to snuff the air.
Then war brought down his fist, and missed the pair!
Yet Hoad was scratched by a splinter, the blood came,
And out burst terrors that he'd striven to tame,
A good man, Hoad, for weeks. *I'm blown to bits*
He groans, he screams. *Come, Bluffer, where's your wits?*
Says Worley, *Bluffer, you've a blighty, man!*
All in the pillbox urged him, here began
His freedom: *Think of Eastbourne and your dad.*
The poor man lay at length and brief and mad
Flung out his cry of doom; soon ebbed and dumb
He yielded. Worley with a tot of rum
And shouting in his face could not restore him.
The ship of Charon over channel bore him.
All marvelled even on that most deathly day
To see this life so spirited away.

THE PROPHET

It is a country,
Says this old guide-book to the Netherlands,
—Written when Waterloo was hardly over,
And justified "a warmer interest
In English travellers" — Flanders is a country
Which, boasting not "so many natural beauties"
As others, yet has history enough.
I like the book; it flaunts the polished phrase
Which our forefathers practised equally
To bury admirals or sell beaver hats;
Let me go on, and note you here and there
Words with a difference to the likes of us.
The author "will not dwell on the temptations
Which many parts of Belgium offer"; he
"Will not insist on the salubrity
Of the air." I thank you, sir, for those few words.
With which we find ourselves in sympathy.
And here are others: "here the unrivalled skill
Of British generals, and the British soldier's
Unconquerable valour..." no, not us.
Proceed.
"The necessary cautions on the road" ...
Gas helmets at the alert, no daylight movement?
"But lately much attention has been paid
To the coal mines." Amen, roars many a fosse
Down south, and slag-heap unto slag-heap calls.
"The Flemish farmers are likewise distinguished
For their attention to manure." Perchance.
First make your mixen, then about it raise
Your tenements; let the house and sheds and sties
And arch triumphal opening on the mud
Inclose that Mecca in a square. The fields,
Our witness saith, are for the most part small,
And "leases are unfortunately short,"
In this again perceive veracity;
At Zillebeke the cultivator found
That it was so; and Fritz, who thought to settle

Down by Verbrandenmolen, came with spades
And dropped his spades, and ran more dead than alive.
Nor, to disclose a secret, do I languish
For lack of a long lease on Pilkem Ridge.

While in these local hints, I cannot wait
But track the author on familiar ground.
He comes from Menin, names the village names
That since rang round the world, leaves Zillebeke,
Crosses a river (so he calls that blood-leat
Bassevillebeek), a hill (a hideous hill),
And reaches Ypres, "pleasant, well-built town."
My Belgian Traveller, did no threatening whisper
Sigh to you from the hid profound of fate
Ere you passed thence, and noted "Poperinghe.
Traffic in serge and hops"? (The words might still
Convey sound fact). Perhaps some dim hush envoy
Entered your spirit when at Furnes you wrote,
"The air is reckoned unhealthy here for strangers."
I find your pen, as driven by irony's fingers,
Defend the incorrectness of your map
With this: it was not fitting to delay,
Though "in a few weeks a new treaty of Paris
Would render it useless." Good calm worthy man,
I leave you changing horses, and I wish you
Good *blanc* at Nieuport. — Truth did not disdain
This sometime seer, crass but Cassandra-like.

VLAMERTINGHE: PASSING THE CHATEAU, JULY 1917

"And all her silken flanks with garlands drest" —
But we are coming to the sacrifice.
Must those have flowers who are not yet gone West?
May those have flowers who live with death and lice?
This must be the floweriest place
That earth allows; the queenly face
Of the proud mansion borrows grace for grace
Spite of those brute guns lowing at the skies.

Bold great daisies, golden lights,
Bubbling roses' pinks and whites —
Such a gay carpet! poppies by the million;
Such damask! such vermilion!
But if you ask me, mate, the choice of colour
Is scarcely right; this red should have been much duller.

CONCERT PARTY: BUSSEBOOM

The stage was set, the house was packed,
    The famous troop began;
Our laughter thundered, act by act;
    Time light as sunbeams ran.

Dance sprang and spun and neared and fled,
    Jest chirped at gayest pitch,
Rhythm dazzled, action sped
    Most comically rich.

With generals and lame privates both
    Such charms worked wonders, till
The show was over – lagging loth
    We faced the sunset chill;

And standing on the sandy way,
    With the cracked church peering past,
We heard another matinée,
    We heard the maniac blast

Of barrage south by Saint Eloi,
    And the red lights flaming there
Called madness: Come, my bonny boy,
    And dance to the latest air.

To this new concert, white we stood;
    Cold certainty held our breath;
While men in the tunnels below Larch Wood
    Were kicking men to death.

ANOTHER JOURNEY FROM BETHUNE TO CUINCHY

I see you walking
To a pale petalled sky,
And the green silent water
Is resting there by;
It seems like bold madness
But that "you" is I.

I long to interpret
That voice of a bell
So silver and simple,
Like a wood-dove-egg shell,
On the bank where you are walking —
It was I heard it well.

At the lock the sky bubbles
Are dancing and dying,
Some the smallest of pearls,
Some moons, and all flying,
Returning, and melting —
You watched them, half-crying.

This is Marie-Louise,
You need not have told me —
I remember her eyes
And the Cognac she sold me —
It is you that are sipping it;
Even so she cajoled me.

Her roof and her windows
Were nothing too sound,
And here and there holes
Some forty feet round
(Antiquer than Homer)
Encipher the ground.

Do you jib at my tenses?
Who's who? You or I?
Do you own Bethune
And that grave eastward sky?
Bethune is miles off now,
'Ware wire and don't die.

The telegraph posts
Have revolted at last,
And old Perpendicular
Leans to the blast,
The rigging hangs ragging
From each plunging mast.

What else would you fancy,
For here it is war?
My thanks, you young upstart,
I've been here before —
I know this Division,
And hate this damned Corps.

"Kingsclere" hath its flowers,
And piano to boot;
The coolest of cellars —
— Your finest salute!
You fraudulent wretch —
You appalling recruit!

O haste, for the darnel
Hangs over the trench,
As yellow as the powder
Which kills with a stench!
Shall you or I go?
O I'll go — don't mench!

But both of us slither
Between the mossed banks,
And through thirsty chalk

Where the red-hatted cranks
Have fixed a portcullis
With notice-board — thanks!

A mad world, my masters!
Whose masters? my lad,
If you are not I
It is I who am mad;
Let's report to the company,
Your mess, egad.

Well, now sir (though lime juice
Is nothing to aid),
This young fellow met me,
And kindly essayed
To guide me — but now it seems
I am betrayed.

He says he is I,
And that I am not he;
But the same omened sky
Led us both, we agree, —
If we cannot commingle,
Pray take him and me.

For where the numb listener
Lies in the dagged weed,
I'll see your word law,
And this youth has agreed
To let me use *his* name —
Take the will for the deed.

And what if the whistle
Of the far-away train
Comes moan-like through mist
Over Coldstream Lane,
Come mocking old love
Into waking again?

And the thinkings of life,
Whether those of thy blood,
Or the manifold soul
Of field and of flood —
What if they come to you
Bombed in the mud?

Well, now as afore
I should wince so, no doubt,
And still to my star
I should cling, all about,
And muddy one midnight
We all will march out.

— Sir, this man may talk,
But he surely omits
That a crump any moment
May blow us to bits;
On this rock his identity –
Argument splits.

I see him walking
In a golden-green ground,
Where pinafored babies
And skylarks abound,
But that's his own business.
My time for trench round.

AN INFANTRYMAN

Painfully writhed the last few weeds upon those houseless
   uplands,
      Cleft pods had dropt their blackened seeds into the
         trampled clay,
Wind and rain were running loose, and icy flew the whiplash;
      Masked guns like autumn thunder drummed the outcast
         year away.

Hidden a hundred yards ahead with winter's blinding passion,
      The mule-beat track appeared half dead, even war's hot
         blood congealed;
The half-dug trenches brimmed like troughs, the camps lay
   slushed and empty,
      Unless those bitter whistlings proved Death's army in the
         field.

Over the captured ridge above the hurt battalion waited,
      And hardly had sense left to prove if ghost or living passed
From hole to hole with sunken eyes and slow ironic orders,
      While fiery fountains burst and clanged — and there your
         lot was cast.

Yet I saw your health and youth go brightening to the vortex,
      The ghosts on guard, the storm uncouth were then no
         match for you;
You smiled, you sang, your courage rang, and to this day I hear it,
      Sunny as a May-day dance, along that spectral avenue.

PREMATURE REJOICING

What's that over there?
                              Thiepval Wood.
Take a steady look at it; it'll do you good.
Here, these glasses will help you. See any flowers?
There sleeps Titania (correct — the Wood is ours);
There sleeps Titania in a deep dugout,
Waking, she wonders what all the din's about,
And smiles through her tears, and looks ahead ten years,
And sees her Wood again, and her usual Grenadiers,
        All in green,
        Music in the moon;
    That burnt rubbish you've just seen
    Won't beat the Fairy Queen;
        All the same, it's a shade too soon
        For you to scribble rhymes
        In your army book
        About those times;
        Take another look;
    That's where the difficulty is, over there.

INTO THE SALIENT

Sallows like heads in Polynesia,
With few and blood-stuck hairs,
Mud-layered cobble-stones,
Soldiers in smoky sheds, blackening uniforms and walls with
    their cookery;
Shell-holes in roofs, in roads,
Even in advertisements
Of bicycles and beer;
The Middle Ages gone to sleep, and woken up to this —
A salvo, four flat slamming explosions.
When you come out the wrong side of the ruin, you are facing
    Hill Sixty,
Hill Sixty is facing you.
You have been planted on the rim of a volcano,
Which will bring forth its fruit — at any second.
Better to be shielded from these facts;
There is a cellar, or was just now.
If the wreck isn't knocked in on us all,
We may emerge past the two Belgian policemen,
The owners' representatives,
Standing in their capes on the steps of the hollow estaminet
Open at all hours to all the winds
At the Poperinghe end of Ypres.
O if we do, if time will pass in time,
We will march
With rifles butt-upwards, in our teeth, any way you like,
Into seven days of country where you come out any door.

THE MEMORIAL, 1914-1918

Against this lantern, shrill, alone
The wind springs out of the plain.
Such winds as this must fly and moan
Round the summit of every stone
On every hill; and yet a strain
Beyond the measure elsewhere known
Seems here.
             Who cries? who mingles with the gale?
Whose touch, so anxious and so weak, invents
A coldness in the coldness? In this veil
Of whirling mist what hue of clay consents?
Can atoms intercede?

And are those shafted bold constructions there,
Mines more than golden, wheels that outrace need,
Crowded corons, victorious chimneys — are
Those touched with question too? pale with the dream
Of those who in this aether-stream
Are urging yet their painful, wounded theme?

Day flutters as a curtain, stirred
By a hidden hand; the eye grows blurred.
Those towers, uncrystalled, fade.
The wind from the north and east and south
Comes with its starved white mouth
And at this crowning trophy cannot rest —
No, speaks as something past plain words distressed.

Be still, if these your voices are; this monolith
For you and your high sleep was made.
Some have had less.
No gratitude in deathlessness?
No comprehension of the tribute paid?

You would speak still? Who with?

NOVEMBER 1ST 1931

We talked of ghosts; and I was still alive;
And I that very day was thirty-five;
Alone once more, I stared about my room
And wished some ghost would be a friend and come;
I cared not of what shape or semblance; terror
Was nothing in comparison with error;
I wished some ghost would come, to talk of fate,
And tell me why I drove my pen so late,
And help with observations on my knack
Of being always on the bivouac,
Here and elsewhere, for ever changing ground,
Finding and straightway losing what I found,
Baffled in time, fumbling each sequent date,
Mistaking Magdalen for the Menin Gate.
This much I saw without transmortal talk,
That war had quite changed my sublunar walk —
Forgive me, dear, honoured and saintly friends
Ingratitude suspect not; this transcends.
Forgive, O sweet red-smiling love, forgive,
If this is life, for your delight I live;
How every lamp, how every pavement flames
Your beauty at me, and your faith acclaims!
But from my silences your kindness grew,
And I surrendered for the time to you,
And still I hold you glorious and my own,
I'd take your hands, your lips; but I'm alone.
So I was forced elsewhere, and would accost
For colloquy and guidance some kind ghost.
As one that with a serious trust was sent
Afar, and bandits seized him while he went,
And long delayed, so I; I yearned to catch
What I should know before my grave dispatch
Was to be laid before that General
Who in a new Time cries "backs to the wall".
No ghost was granted me; and I must face
Uncoached the masters of that Time and Space,
And there with downcast murmurings set out
What my gross late appearance was about.

THE LOST BATTALION

"To dream again". That chance. There were no fences,
No failures, no impossibles, no tenses.
Here's the huge sulky ship, the captain's room,
The swilling decks like hillsides, the iron boom
Of ocean's pugilism, black faces, low
Corner-cabals — "Where are we bound? D'ye know?"
And now, long months being drummed into our lives,
The bells ring back and fro, the boat arrives —
We've seen this place, does no one know its *name?*
Name missing. But we'll get there all the same.
It's all the same. I thought the war was done.
We'll have to hurry, the Battalion's gone.
How on again? Only an Armistice.
I thought my nerves weren't quite so bad as this.
That white house hangs on strangely, turn sharp right,
And the instant war spreads gray and mute in sight.
I feel my old gear on my back, and know
My general job in this forthcoming show;
But what's the catch, the difference? Someone speak!
Name wanted, or I shan't get there this week.

AT RUGMER

Among sequestered farms and where brown orchards
Weave in the thin and coiling wind, and where
The pale cold river ripples still as moorhens
Work their restless crossing,
Among such places, when October warnings
Sound from each kex and thorn and shifting leaf,
We well might wander, and renew some stories
Of a dim time when we were kex and thorn,
Sere leaf, ready to hear a hissing wind
Whip down and wipe us out; our season seemed
At any second closing.
So, we were wrong. But we have lived this landscape,
And have an understanding with these shades.

TO WILFRED OWEN
Killed in action November 4th, 1918

Where does your spirit walk, kind soldier, now,
In this deep winter, bright with ready guns?
And have you found new poems in this war?

Some would more wish you, with untroubled brow,
Perpetual sleep, which you perhaps wished once —
To unknow this swift return of all you bore.

And yet, if ever in the scheme of things
Past men have leave to see the world they loved,
This night you crossed the lines, for a second seen

By worried sentries. In vast tunnellings
You track the working-party; by the gloved
Wire-sergeant stand; look in at the canteen;

And I, dream-following you, reading your eyes,
Your veteran youthful eyes, discover fair
Some further hope, which did not formerly rise.
Smiling you fade, the future meets you there.

BY THE BELGIAN FRONTIER

"Where youth in fires
Fiend-blown, fiend-sudden, strove and fell,
The lilac sunlight plays like sweet desires,
The new leaves melodize, and the winds tune well,
The far tower's bell answers the browsing-bell.

"The twentieth year
Is now fulfilled, the lands of nourished strength
Warm-bodied give us welcome with their yield
Of flax blue-flowered and white. The placid length
Of the crystal lake lies like a war-god's shield,
Fallen for boys to find while flying kites afield."

So even this spring
I wrote, I stared with never a wild surmise
Near that old frontier. Now the hideous thing
Is loose again, the ready death-forms rise.

HOME, FAMILY, REFLECTIONS

SICK BED

Half dead with fever here in bed I sprawl,
In candlelight watching the odd flies crawl
Across the ceiling's bleak white desolation; —
Can they not yet have heard of gravitation? —
Hung upside down above the precipice
To doze the night out; ignorance is bliss!
Your blood be on your head, ridiculous flies.

Dizzying with these, I glare and tantalise
At the motley hides of books which moulder here:
'On Choosing A Career', 'Ten Thousand a Year';
'Ellis on Sheep', 'Lamb's Tales', a doleful Gay,
A has-been Young, dead 'Lives', vermilion Gray,
And a whole corps of 1790 twelves.
My eye goes blurred along these gruesome shelves,
My brain whirs 'Poems of...Poems of...' like a clock;
And I stare for my life at the square black ebony block
Of darkness in the open window-frame.
Then my thoughts flash in one white searching flame
On my little lost daughter; I gasp and grasp to see
Her shy smile pondering out who I might be,
Her rathe-ripe rounded cheeks, near-violet eyes.
Long may I stare; her stony Fate denies
The vision of her, though tired Fancy's sight
Scrawl with pale curves the dead and scornful night.

All the night's full of questing flights and calls
Of owls and bats, white owls from time-struck walls,
Bats with their shrivelled speech and dragonish wings.
Beneath, a strange step crunches the ash path where
None goes so late, I know: the mute vast air
Wakes to a great sigh.
                          Now the murmurings,
Cricks, rustlings, knocks, all forms of tiny sound
That have long been happening in my room half-heard,
Grow fast and fierce, each one a ghostly word.

76

I feel the grutching pixies hedge me round;
"Folly", sneers courage (and flies). Stealthily creaks
The threshold, fingers fumble, terror speaks,
And, bursting into sweats I muffle deep
My face in pillows, praying for merciful sleep.

THE CHILD'S GRAVE

I came to the churchyard where pretty Joy lies
  On a morning in April, a rare sunny day;
Such bloom rose around, and so many birds' cries,
  That I sang for delight as I followed the way.

I sang for delight in the ripening of spring,
  For dandelions even were suns come to earth;
Not a moment went by but a new lark took wing
  To wait on the season with melody's mirth.

Love-making birds were my mates all the road,
  And who would wish surer delight for the eye
Than to see pairing goldfinches gleaming abroad
  Or yellowhammers sunning on paling and sty?

And stocks in the almswomen's garden were blown
  With rich Easter roses each side of the door;
The lazy white owls in the glade cool and lone
  Paid calls on their cousins in the elm's chambered core.

This peace, then, and happiness thronged me around.
  Nor could I go burdened with grief, but made merry
Till I came to the gate of that overgrown ground
  Where scarce once a year sees the priest come to bury.

Over the mounds stood the nettles in pride,
  And, where no fine flowers, there kind weeds dared
      to wave;
It seemed but as yesterday she lay by my side,
  And now my dog ate of the grass on her grave.

He licked my hand wondering to see me muse so,
  And wished I would lead on the journey or home,
As though not a moment of spring were to go
  In brooding; but I stood, if her spirit might come

And tell me her life, since we left her that day
   In the white lilied coffin, and rained down our tears;
But the grave held no answer, though long I should stay;
   How strange that this clay should mingle with hers!

So I called my good dog, and went on my way;
   Joy's spirit shone then in each flower I went by,
And clear as the noon, in coppice and ley,
   Her sweet dawning smile and her violet eye!

TO JOY

Is not this enough for moan
To see this babe all motherless —
A babe beloved — thrust out alone
    Upon death's wilderness?
Our tears fall, fall, fall — I would weep
My blood away to make her warm,
Who never went on earth one step,
    Nor heard the breath of the storm.
How shall you go, my little child,
Alone on that most wintry wild?

A "FIRST IMPRESSION" (TOKYO)

No sooner was I come to this strange roof,
Beyond broad seas, half round the weary world,
Than came the pretty ghost, the sudden-sweet
And most sad spirit of my vanished child:
From the bare corners of the unknown room
She peeped with beauty's eyes, till my eyes rained
Their helpless tears once more; and there, and there
Was my dead baby baffling with dream presence,
And singing, till I thought I must be mad –
Was not all silent? yet, I heard her song.
Child, will not Orcus yield you? that small voice
Wafts, as I know, from where I cannot come
And that smile glimmers like the ethereal flowers
In your far meadows; would that earth's kind flowers
Might now be golden in your toddling path!

Thus moved my musings, till at length I heard
From neighbouring doors slid back along their grooves
Small children scurrying, with the hastiest joy,
And quick young voices planning glorious play;
I looked, and saw some in their dresses bright
Laying themselves a garden in the dust,
With broad green leaves to be their noble trees,
With beds marked out, and buds desired to grow.
Oh, millions, millions in this world (I cried)
Are the glad children blossoming fast and fair,
Filling both homes and homeless hearts with airs
Of young eternity; and other worlds
Had their child millions too, so kind in this
Is nature; and though one of these dear blooms
Fall, still great childhood lords it all the way,
And the whole earth may see and hear and glory.

The children shouted as this way and that
They hurried, and I glittered with their light,
And loved them, as if kindred of my own,
And felt deep faith in nature's motherhood.
To me, were not two younglings given and spared?
I saw them in the Suffolk lane; high flowed
A tide of love and surety in my breast.
But still, I saw a ghost, and lacked one child.

A DREAM

Unriddle this. Last night my dream
Took me along a sullen stream,
A water drifting black and ill,
With idiot swirls, and silent still.
As if it had been Pactolus
And I of gold sands amorous
I went determined on its bank,
Stopped in that breath of dim and dank,
And in my hand (in dream's way) took
A living fish to bait my hook,
A living fish, not gudgeon quite
Nor dace nor roach, a composite.
Then ghoulishly with fingers, yet
With aching mind I strove to get
The pang of shackling metal through
The mouth of that poor mad perdu,
And (ran the bitter fancy's plot)
To tie his body in a knot.
While thus I groped and grasped and coiled
And he in horror flapped and foiled,
I saw how on the clay around
Young shining fishes leapt and clowned,
And often turned their eyes on me,
Begging their watery liberty,
Most sad and odd. But, thought I, now
I have no time for helping you.
And then at length my bait was hooked,
His shuddering tail grotesquely crooked:
Black was the secret-dimpling stream,
I flounced him to the line's extreme.
And then, his mercy, gladdening me
Who just had been his agony,
Some monstrous mouth beat out his brain,
The line cut wide its graphs of strain.
I knew my prize, and fought my best
With thought and thew — then the fight ceased.
Sobbing I feared the quarry gone,

83

But no, the deadweight showed him on,
Slow to the mould I pulled the huge
Half-legend from his subterfuge,
And as he from the water thrust
His head, and cleared its scurf and must,
Two eyes as old as Adam stared
On mine. And now he lay unbared:
My glory! — On the bleak bank lay
A carcass effigy in clay,
A trunk of vague and lethal mass
Such as might lie beneath filmed glass,
Where on the pane the buzzing fly
Batters to win the desperate sky.

THE ESCAPE

In the stubble blossoms
    A pansy small,
Which I will get and set again
    Beneath my house wall.

I took the tiny outlaw
    I gave it sheltered ground;
In the stubble blooms a pansy now,
    But here no sign is found.

VALUES

Till darkness lays a hand on these gray eyes
And out of man my ghost is sent alone,
It is my chance to know that force and size
Are nothing but by answered undertone.
No beauty even of absolute perfection
Dominates here — the glance, the pause, the guess
Must be my amulets of resurrection;
Raindrops may murder, lightnings may caress.

There I was tortured, but I cannot grieve;
There crowned and palaced — visibles deceive.
That storm of belfried cities in my mind
Leaves me my vespers cool and eglantined.
From love's wide-flowering mountain-side I chose
This sprig of green, in which an angel shows.

THE KISS

I am for the woods against the world,
  But are the woods for me?
I have sought them sadly anew, fearing
  My fate's mutability,
Or that which action and process make
  Of former sympathy.

Strange that those should arrive strangers
  Who were once entirely at home.
Colonnade, sunny wall and warren,
  Islet, osier, foam,
Buds and leaves and selves seemed
  Safe to the day of doom.

By-roads following, and this way wondering,
  I spy men abroad
In orchards, knarred and woody men
  Whose touch is bough and bud;
Co-arboreal sons of landscape.
  Then in the windstript wood

Is the cracking of stems; and under the thorn
  With a kobold's closeness lurks
The wanderer with his knife and rods,
  That like a bald rook works;
His woman-rook about the thicket
  Prowls at the hazel-forks.

Sheep lying out by the swollen river
  Let the flood roll down
Without so much as a glance; they know it;
  The hurling seas of brown
Cannot persuade the ferrying moorhen
  Her one willow will drown.

This way wondering, I renew
    Some sense of common right;
And through my armour of imposition
    Win the Spring's keen light,
Till for the woods against the world
    I kiss the aconite.

ANOTHER ALTAR

I am Forgetfulness. I am that shadow
Of whom well warned you thought your pathway clear.
You need sharp eyes to catch such silent shadows.
Not all your wakeful plans and resolution
Outsoldiered me; you heard me at last low-laughing,
"When the steed's stolen, shut the stable door".
This, too, is nothing of mine. No sly ambition
Nor malice moves me; but my part is fixed
In changing onward life from scene to scene,
Necessitating futures of surprise
Solving some enigmas, much preserving
To bloom a wonder in a way the sowers
Could never have guessed. I touch the cells of the mind,
And some are by that finger barred and bolted;
It may be but a moment that I triumph;
Consider what my moments still achieve.
Through me the wife learns who the mistress is,
And where. I trap the assassin, and safe murder
Becomes a dance on air. One look from me
And the mind's eye of the signalman is dimmed
And wreckage piles and flames above the dead.
I have contrived that some most secret treasures
Shall lie an age untouched, and late-discovered
Should be the source of hope and peace; I leave
A child's toy to become posterity's marvel,
From lost Tanagra; this quaint poniard lurked
Under my influences, where the culprit stowed it,
To tell man something of his martyrdoms,
Upon a day. From these my hoarded papers
At length uncovered, an impoverished fame
Grows full and noon-day clear; with that, your scholar
Is charmed with joys not his, and shall not fail
Of praise and proud remembrance — while I will.
Be sure, unsure of most, that I will make
An instrument of you this very day,

That I may weave my share of Then and Now,
A web that greater gods design – with me.
He that now writes the words I whisper to him
Has here and there unknowingly surrendered
To my caprice, if so he please to style it,
And will still find his early morning again,
Through me, after a dry and drouthy journey,
All fresh and violet-dewy; he, at least,
Will not disdain to bow to me as one
Among the more ingenious undergods.

MENTAL HOSPITAL
II: POOR TOM'S WELCOME

Along the rows the party goes,
    Along the rows of withered men,
The girls with perfumed flower-like clothes,
The youths whose strength's the strength of ten —
        And humbly sit those withered men
        The slow ones, in their den.

They see the raree-show float by,
    They eye it with no wild concern —
It will go by; it's bright enough,
But there's no seizing such cloud-stuff.
        One roars his sudden loud return
        To old ways, then stops stern.

But one there is who cannot stay
    Unmoved; the dwarf he leaves his chair,
And shuffling works his apeish way
To the strangers; and with smiling air
        And no word said, holds out his hand
        And looks his *you will understand*.

They take his hand, now that, now this,
    And he smiles on; and then they're past.
Done is the courtesy, cold the bliss.
He sinks away as a dead leaf cast
        Into some slack grey pool; the light
        Was brief, how long the night!

A TALE NOT IN CHAUCER
(not even in Dryden's Chaucer)

In France, no matter what the Town, there stood
A Convent, justly fam'd for doing good,
Where ev'ry day just twenty paupers ate
A Dinner giv'n 'em freely at the Gate.
A Dog there was, who noticed this Regale,
And join'd the Crew each day with wagging Tail.
But they were hungry Gents; the luckless Beast
Got nothing but th'Aroma of the Feast.
Now mark, each Portion was deliver'd thus:
A Serving-man remain'd within the House
And plac'd the Food within a round machine,
And turn'd it outward; 'twas receiv'd unseen.
All this upon the ringing of a Bell.
The Dog discover'd he could toll it well,
And one Day when th' unshaven Sort had din'd
He siez'd the Rope, which work'd as he design'd;
The turn'd machine display'd the wish'd-for Roast,
The grinning Rogue approv'd and no Time lost.
And the next Day and ev'ry Day he came,
The same Bell pull'd and gain'd his meal the same.
But what in this vain world is permanent?
The Cook within with Grief observ'd, there went
Twenty-one Portions from his Grill each Day,
And Twenty was laid down. 'O let me lay,
Almighty God, the villain by the Heels
Who thus extends this Privilege of meals.'
He lurks, and looks. — The twenty Hoboes pass'd
And grabb'd their Grub. The twentieth was the last.
Only a Dog remain'd, and what of that?
And yet the Animal seem'd strangely fat.
Monsieur reflected, and Suspicion grew:
The Dog before his Eyes rose, rang and drew
A mighty Plateful of the Convent's Beef.
Away went Cook, to state the Case and Thief.
But the Community with Pleasure heard,

And deem'd th' ingenious Dog should have Reward,
And order'd that each Day his heap'd-up Plate
Should be supply'd him when he call'd for that;
The Pensioner well pleas'd maintain'd his Place,
And dy'd the Father of a num'rous Race.

MINORITY REPORT

That you have given us others endless means
To modify the dreariness of living,
Machines which even change men to machines;
That you have been most honourable in giving;
That thanks to you we roar through space at speed
Past dreams of wisest science not long since,
And listen in to news we hardly need,
And rumours which might make Horatius wince,
Of modes of sudden death devised by you,
And promising protection against those –
All this and more I know, and what is due
Of praise would offer, couched more fitly in prose.
But such incompetence and such caprice
Clog human nature that, for all your kindness,
Some shun loud-speakers as uncertain peace,
And fear flood-lighting is a form of blindness;
The televisionary world to come,
The petrol-driven world already made,
Appear not to afford these types a crumb
Of comfort. You will win; be not dismayed.
Let those pursue their fantasy, and press
For absolute illusion, let them seek
Mere moonlight in the last green loneliness;
Your van will be arriving there next week.

WRITING A SKETCH OF A FORGOTTEN POET

Here this great summer day,
    While the fields are wild
With flowers you name, I stay,
    And have learnedly compiled

From shaky books, too few,
    Dry registers,
Something of the living you;
    And have gleaned your verse.

You might have laughed to see,
    With this rich sun,
One pent in a library
    Who else might run

Free in the flashing sweet
    Life-lavishing air.
Or, lover of books, you'd greet
    Such constancy and care.

You might have laughed to hear
    Your stanzas read –
If it were not so clear
    The dead are dead.

What gulfs between us lie!
    I had thought them crossed,
Dreaming to gratify
    Your unimpatient ghost.

CHAFFINCH
On Suburban Growths

"Gone down, Sir, and whatever bird you speak to
That really knows these parts will open his beak to
Support my view; the place is *going down*".
He paused, and frowned, if chaffinches may frown.
"This very street you're standing in confirms
The fact that time gets worse for birds and worms.
There was a day, before these fancy gents
Sent up at once their buildings and their rents
When Hadrian Avenue was Squandering Lane.
As things are now, a pretty shower of rain
Is wasted; this high-polished surface throws
The water off so fast, one hardly knows
There's been a drop. Before these patent makes,
In the old track it used to lie like lakes,
And bathing birds, perhaps ten tens together,
Came down to dip and frill and fresh each feather.
Yes, in those days roadmakers could make roads,
Ask, if you don't believe me, frogs and toads,
Lizards and newts, — if they were here today,
They'd pay no calls the other side o' the way.
Myself, I never saw such lovely dust
As we had here, before that Housing Trust —
Blackbirds or gray birds, sparrows, jenny-wrens,
Would come in quiet sun to chatter and cleanse;
And I could mention brambles, blackthorns, sedge,
A crab-tree and two snub-oaks in the hedge, —
Where, just where you are looking, at that date
Two hedgehogs justified the married state.
I did not mean, dear sir, to make you cry;
With all these people passing by;
In fact, I had forgotten — I had best
Be off, or be bumped off, like all the rest."

THE KIND STAR

You must be as others are;
Puzzled, clouded, even afraid.
Still, you seem to have a star
Lighting you with certainty,
Companying you constantly,
Deathless in conservancy
While others run dismayed.

So to me, sweet you, you are
Heavenly message, moving here;
You become my gentle star.
Look, and all my prowlings clear;
Speak, and desperation dies;
Come my way, and fury flies;
Joy, and man's huge chaos lies
Calm in calm atmosphere.

THE SUM OF ALL

So rise, enchanting haunting faithful
Music of life recalled and now revealing
Unity; now discerned beyond
Fear, obscureness, casualty,
Exhaustion, shame and wreck,
As what was best,
As what was deeply well designed.
So rise, as a clear hill road with steady ascension,
Issuing from drifted outskirts, huddled houses,
Casual inns where guests may enter and wait
Many a moment till the hostess find them;
Thence ever before the carter, passing the quarries,
The griffin-headed gateways,
Windmill, splashing rill, derelict sheepfold,
Tower of a thousand years —
Through the pinewoods,
Where warm stones lodge the rose-leaf butterfly;
Crossing the artillery ranges whose fierce signs
Mean nothing now, whose gougings look like
Bird-baths now; and last, the frontier farm
And guard-house made of bracken.
Rising to this old eyrie, quietly forsaken,
You bear me on, and not me only.
All difference sheds away,
All shrivelling of the sense, anxious prolepsis,
Injury, staring suspicion,
Fades into pure and wise advance.
So rise; so let me pass.

GOD'S TIME

A gentler heaven steals over the hour,
      And at its pace I go
And scan green things that grow
      Beneath old hedge and ivy-bower.
Most gracious falls the silent hour.

Through the shut sky an eye of blue
      Twinkles upon the soul,
Even as these weeds unroll
      Their leaves aspiring, choice and new;
Their greenness blesses, and that blue.

The round leaf, shield leaf, patterned spray
      All shine like love's first tears,
And though no primrose peers,
      Nor aconites, nor windflowers play,
I have their message through leaf and spray.

This may not be the hour I supposed
      When from the house I came
Informed of a world aflame;
      That will have been an era closed,
Though endless as I then supposed.

O green leaves born in winter's heart,
      White ghosts of flowers to be,
Come here so quietly,
And blossoming heaven's blue counterpart,
      — I have lost my way, and found my heart.

HIGH ELMS, BRACKNELL

Two buds we took from thousands more
In Shelley's garden overgrown,
Beneath our roof they are now full-blown,
A royal pair, a scarlet twain
Through whose warm lives our thoughts explore
Back through long years to come at one
Which Shelley loved in sun or rain.

Fleeting's the life of these strange flowers,
Enchanting poppies satin-frilled,
Dark-purple hearts, yet these rebuild
A distant world, a summer dead
Millions of poppy-lives ere ours,
And Shelley's visionary towers
Come nearer in their Indian red;

Not but some shadow of despair
In this dark purple ominous
From that high summer beckons us;
And such a shadow, such a doom
Was lurking in the garden there.
We could not name the incubus,
Save that it haunted Shelley's home.

Was it that through the same glass door
With weary heart, uncertain why,
But first discerning love can die,
Harriet had moved alone and slow;
Or Shelley in the moonlight bore
The cold curt word Necessity
From poppies that had seemed to know?

Then tracing the lost path between
The herbs and flowers and wilderness,
Whose was the phantom of our guess
Drawn by that quiet deserted pond
With little boat, now scarcely seen
For tears or bodings? Whose distress
Darkened the watery diamond?

DOG ON WHEELS

This dog — not a real dog, you know, —
An Airedale, on four wheels, —
Not *my* toy, but a friend of mine as things go,
Is alone; we leave to the rest their reels.
I speak to him, he seems to hear.
His face is a little battered now,
And so is mine: to Change both bow.
Let that be: with vision I dream to endow
This dog on wheels.
                          Poor dear,
Can such things be? Not so.
We are simple, and that uplifted face
Is of its own kind in time and space.
But as I shut my desk and say goodbye,
Downward droops a disappointed eye.

THE FAR EAST

EASTERN TEMPEST

That flying angel's torrent cry
Will hurl the mountains through the sky!
A wind like fifty winds at once
Through the bedragoned kingdom runs,
An army of rain slants icy stings
At many a wretch afield who clings
His cloak of straw, with glistening spines
Like a prodigious porcupine's.
The reptile grasses by his path
Wind sleek as unction from that Wrath
Which with a glassy claw uproots
The broad-leaved *kiri*, flays and loots
Torn and snarled sinews, leaves for dead
The young crops with the shining head,
While blotched blunt melons darkly dot
The slaughtered swathes like cannon-shot.
The lotus in each pond upheaves
Its sacred, slow, appealing leaves,
And many a bush with wrestling jerk
Defies the daemon's murderous work —
Yet nature stares white-lipped, to read
In Chance's eye what desperate deed?
    A kinder god discerns, replies,
And stills the land's storm-shouts to sighs:
The clouds in massy folds apart
Disclose the day's bright bleeding heart,
Huge plumes and scarves black-tossing wide
As if a Kubla Khan had died!
From flame to flame the vision glows,
Till all the pools of heaven unclose
The lotus-light, the hue, the balm
Of wisdom infinitely calm.

A JAPANESE EVENING

Round us the pines are darkness
That with a wild melodious piping rings
While in the ditches
Slow as toads in English gardens
The little landcrabs move.
We re-discover our path,
And, coming to the cottage, are greeted
With hierophantic usherings and oracles,
And a grin behind the screen, I imagine.
We guess full fathom five, and take up the chopsticks.
The metal-blue cucumber slices,
Rice, string beans,
And green tea over,
The housekeeper looking kindly amazement
At the master of the house
Soon makes all shipshape.
After all, they possess an American clock,
A very fine, a high-collar clock.
She sits on the mat, awaiting the next oddity.

Lanterns moon the outer darkness,
And merrily in come floating
(So gently they foot the honourable straw)
Three young girls, who sit them down.
A conference:
Almost the Versailles of the Far East:
The master, beaming,
His white hair in the lamplight seeming brighter with his
        pleasure,
Asks me what I call *O tsuki sama*.
Moon.
Mooon.
Moon.
He has got it; right first time,
But not the next.

Moooni.
(The housekeeper cannot suppress her giggles,
Okashii, she says, and so it is.)
We now pass naturally to the
Electric Light.
But he will not have that,
There are no things like that in heaven and earth
In his philology.
I repeat – what I said;
He repeats – what he said.
We close at Erecturiku Rightu.
We fasten also on:
The cat, who becomes catsu,
The dog, who proceeds doggi,
(And I suspect has rabies beginning);
Himself, O-Ji-San, Orudu Genturuman,
And all sorts of enigmas.

The girls are quicker, more nimble-throated
And will reproduce exactly the word, but he lays the law
        down;
Having re-orientated Fan
Which they pronounced Fan,
Into Weino,
He instructs then how it ought to be pronounced,
Obediently young Japan re-iterates his decision,
Not without an ocular hint to the stranger
That they have concealed the other rendering in their
        minds...
I hear their voices tinkling, lessening
Over the firefly grass,
Along the seething sand below the pines,
At the end of the entertainment.

AFTER THE BOMBING

My hesitant design it was, in a time when no man feared,
To make a poem on the last poor flower to have grown on the
    patch of land
Where since a gray enormous stack of shops and offices
    reared
Its bulk as though to eternity there to stand.

Moreover I dreamed of a lyrical verse to welcome another
    flower,
The first to blow on that hidden site when the concrete block
    should cease
Gorging the space; it could not be mine to foretell the means,
    the hour,
But nature whispered something of a longer lease.

We look from the street now over a breezy wilderness of
    bloom,
Now, crowding its colours between the sills and cellars, hosts
    of flame
And foam, pearl-pink and thunder-red, befriending the
    makeshift tomb
Of a most ingenious but impermanent claim.

AN ISLAND TRAGEDY

Among the twinkling-treetops on our hill —
It was perhaps an afternoon illusion —
Above, I saw poised absolutely still
A wood-god, a giant earth-god, — no confusion
At least to my awakened sight: he stood
Head and shoulders aloft the far-off green,
The steady straw-haired monarch of the wood,
As one defending his disturbed demesne.

What was he if not *he*? I used my eyes,
There that Form stood, as ancient as that hill;
He had no right to strike with such surprise
Me! There he stood, for me he always will,
Poor giant, poor doomed straw-hair, staring down
From his starved rock towards the advancing town.

A HONG KONG HOUSE

"And now a dove and now a dragon-fly
Came to the garden; sometimes as we sat
Outdoors in twilight noiseless owl and bat
        Flew shadowily by.
It was no garden, — so adust, red-dry
The rock-drift soil was, no kind root or sweet
Scent-subtle flower would house there, but I own
            At certain seasons, burning bright,
            Full-blown,
Some trumpet-purple blooms blazed at the sun's
                                            huge light."

And then? Tell more.
"The handy lizard and quite nimble toad
            Had courage often to explore
            Our large abode.
The infant lizard whipped across the wall
To his own objects; how to slide like him
Along the upright plane and never fall,
            Ascribe to Eastern whim.
The winged ants flocked to our lamp, and shed
Their petally wings, and walked and crept instead.

"The palm-tree top soared into the golden blue
            And soaring skyward drew
Its straight stem etched with many rings,
And one broad holm-like tree whose name
                        I never knew
Was decked through all its branches with
                        broidering leaves
Of pattern-loving creepers; fine warblings
And gong-notes thence were sounded at our eaves
By clever birds one very seldom spied,
Except when they, of one tree tired,
Into another new-desired,
Over the lawn and scattered playthings chose to glide."

ENDINGS

A SWAN, A MAN

Among the dead reeds, the single swan
Floats and explores the water-shallow under,
While the wet whistling wind blows on
And the path by the river is all alone,
And I at the old bridge wonder
If those are birds or leaves,
Small quick birds or withered leaves,
Astir on the grassy patch of green
Where the wind is not so rough and keen.

What happens to my thought-time,
To my desires, my deeds, this day?
The rainstorm beats the pitiful stream
With battle-pictures I had hoped to miss
But winter warfare could be worse than this;
Into the house, recall what dead friends say,
And like the Ancient Mariner learn to pray.

ANCRE SUNSHINE

In all his glory the sun was high and glowing
Over the farm world where we found great peace,
And clearest blue the winding river flowing
Seemed to be celebrating a release
From all that speed and music of its own
Which but for some few cows we heard alone.

Here half a century before might I,
Had something chanced, about this point have lain,
Looking with failing sense on such blue sky,
And then became a name with others slain.
But that thought vanished. Claire was wandering free
Miraumont way in the golden tasselled lea.

The railway trains went by, and dreamily
I thought of them as planets in their course,
Thought bound perhaps for Arras, how would we
Have wondered once if through the furious force
Murdering our world one of these same had come,
Friendly and sensible — "the war's over, chum".

And now it seemed Claire was afar, and I
Alone, and where she went perhaps the mill
That used to be had risen again, and by
All that had fallen was in its old form still,
For her to witness, with no cold surprise,
In one of those moments when nothing dies.

THE WATCHERS

I heard the challenge "Who goes there?"
Close-kept but mine through midnight air;
I answered and was recognised
And passed, and kindly thus advised:
"There's someone crawlin' through the grass
By the red ruin, or there was,
And them machine guns been a firin'
All the time the chaps was wirin',
So, sir if you're goin' out
You'll keep your 'ead well down no doubt."

When will the stern, fine "Who goes there?"
Meet me again in midnight air?
And the gruff sentry's kindness, when
Will kindness have such power again?
It seems, as now I wake and brood,
And know my hour's decrepitude,
That on some dewy parapet
The sentry's spirit gazes, yet
Who will not speak with altered tone
When I at last am seen and known.

NOTES

Mary Daines, Blunden's first wife, is referred to as Mary. *EB:* Edmund Blunden. *CP:* Notes by EB in Claire Poynting's copy of *Poems 1914-30.* She was EB's third wife. *AH:* Notes by EB in Aki Hayashi's copy of *Undertones of War.* She was EB's secretary in Japan, 1924-27. A romantic attachment ensued. *UW:* 'Undertones of War', (Penguin Classics, 1982 edition).

p.24 THE PREAMBLE
Written 1915, published 1916. From *Pastorals, A Book of Verses* by E.C. Blunden published by Erskine Macdonald, London, June 1916. Appeared in *The Little Books of Georgian Verse – Second Series,* under the general editorship of S. Gertrude Ford, who wrote: "Ten months ago the writer of these poems was a schoolboy at a public school; of whom one of his masters said that he "lived for poetry." He was then senior boy at Christ's Hospital, West Horsham, and a scholar elect of Queen's College, Oxford. Now he has taken a commission in the New Army, and is serving in the 10th Royal Sussex." In 1914 EB arranged for Mr. Price of Horsham to print *Poems,* followed by *The Barn, Three Poems* and *Harbingers.*

p.25 BY CHANCTONBURY
Written 1915, published 1916. *Pastorals* (Erskine Macdonald, 1916). **Chanctonbury** – A wild hill on the Sussex downs, topped with beech trees. It has a reputation for being a mysterious place with malign influences, and the atmosphere of the poem reflects this. The modern, sleek grey lines of the airship provide a contrast with the description of this ancient hill. **knared** – gnarled. **straked** – striped.

p.26 THE BARN
Written 1915, published 1916. "To be had of J. Brooker, High Street, Uckfield, or of G. A. Blunden, Framfield, Uckfield." (from the front page of *The Barn,* published 1916). Alongside *Three Poems* and *Harbingers* this tiny volume was EB's early appearance in print. Quoted on the frontispiece:

"I hate your loathsome Poems"
One Critic.
"Surprisingly mature and original"
Another Critic.

EB sent this chapbook, along with *Harbingers* and *Three Poems*, to Siegfried Sassoon, then literary editor of the *Daily Herald*, in 1919.

p.27 ALMSWOMEN

Written 1918, published 1920. This was first printed in the *London Mercury* and then *The Nation* in 1919; it appeared in *The Waggoner* (Sidgwick and Jackson Ltd., 1920). It was dedicated to Nancy and Robert Graves who EB met when he moved to Oxford as an undergraduate in 1919. The two dames in question lived in Kirtling, Suffolk. EB and Mary – who came from Suffolk – cycled over to see them in the summer of 1918. One was Mary's great aunt and the other her friend. EB wrote the poem that same evening. *CP*: "Composed by way of filling in time at Deve Cottage; the old ladies were actual, and the poem was therefore appreciated when it was read, almost as soon as written down." Deve Cottage was the Daines' family home. **saracens** – onslaught of hailstones.

p.29 MALEFACTORS

Written 1919, published 1920. Published in *The Waggoner*.
orts – fragments.

p.30 NOVEMBER MORNING

Published 1920. First published in *To-day*, June 1920, Vol. 7, No 40, p.138; reprinted (revised) in *The Shepherd*. *CP*: "Congelow again. The shoddy was for the hopgardens." Congelow was the name of a rambling farm house just outside the village of Yalding, Kent, which EB's parents rented from 1904 for a few years when EB was a young boy. **weazen** – variation on 'wizen' meaning shrivelled. **shoddy** – wool from shredded rags. **curry-combs** – for cleaning horses.

p.31 MOLE CATCHER

Published 1920. First published in *The Athenaeum*, 9 July

1920, p.40; reprinted in *The Shepherd*. *CP*: "Once more, much was from Bert Daines's recipe for a good molecatcher." Bert Daines was EB's brother-in-law from his first marriage. EB described Bert as "a repository of Anglian anecdote, fable, dialect and wickedness. He would tell me with perfect contentment whatever he knew of country life and occupation..." (MS in the possession of The Estate of Mrs Claire Blunden). **helved** – helve meaning handle. **lob-worms** – lug or earth worms. **arcanum** – secret remedy or elixir.

p.32 DEATH OF CHILDHOOD BELIEFS
Published 1920. First published in *The Athenaeum*, 8 October 1920; reprinted in *The Shepherd*. *CP*: "Kent is the scene here." **Spider Dick** – probably a local character.

p.34 THE GIANT PUFFBALL
Published 1922. Published in *The Shepherd*. *CP*: "This was from the Newmarket district; the grassland and copses there used to be a paradise of fungi." **churls** – labourers. **haled** – dragged.

p.35 COUNTRY SALE
Published 1922. Published in the *Yale Review* July 1922; then in *A Miscellany of Poetry* edited by William Kean Seymour, (John G. Wilson, December 1922); then in *English Poems* (Cobden-Sanderson 1926). *CP*: "This was a 'sketch from life'. I regret not buying an early Pilgrim's Progress which was among the oddments. Where? Somewhere near Lydgate." EB was a great book collector, with an instinct for where he might find a valuable edition, never wanting to pay more than sixpence. He often found it. **florin** – two shilling piece. **quartern loaf** – a four pound loaf made from a quarter of a stone of flour.

p.37 WINTER: EAST ANGLIA
Published 1923. Published in *To Nature* (The Beaumont Press, 1923). *CP*: "A Jack Daines poem." Jack was one of Mary's brothers who shared EB's love of sport.

p.38 THE MIDNIGHT SKATERS
Published 1925. Published in *Masks of Time* (The Beaumont Press, 1925). *CP*: "Back to Congelow." The setting is rural Kent, but note the use of language appropriate to war – parapet, engines.

p.39 A TRANSCRIPTION
Published 1925. Published in *Masks of Time* 1925. *CP*: "At Bury St. Edmunds."

p.40 THE BAKER'S VAN
Published 1926. Published in *English Poems* (Cobden-Sanderson, 1926). *CP*: "Will Baldock is now, 1954, on the land – and, as I proved by seeing him out at work, he thinks that's incomparable. A wise man, and my friend still." **brown study** – reverie.

p.41 THE MATCH
Published 1928. Published in *Retreat* (Cobden-Sanderson, 1928). *CP*: "Tokyo, 1926." Although the setting is in Japan, this poem is symbolic of something more than the fish and the man facing each other through the glass. The final line seems to take us into another world – that of two opposing sides facing each other across no man's land and the utter futility of trench warfare suffered by his generation. **oeillades** – glances, winks.

p.42 FESTUBERT: THE OLD GERMAN LINE
Written May 1916, published 1930. Published in *Poems 1914-1930* (Cobden-Sanderson, 1930). In the preface to *Poems 1914-30* EB comments as he justifies his choice of poems for that book: "If there were any others that I should like to have had before me in making my choice, they would be the numerous pieces which I remember to have occupied and diverted me in the summer of 1917, while we were making ourselves ready to capture and consolidate the large extent of Belgium then borrowed by Germany. The labours of that summer, however, down to my neat transcripts of 'ode, and elegy, and sonnet,' vanished in the mud." This is one of the few that survived and refers to his first night journey over the

open from the Cover Trench which was "the real front line". This was EB's introduction to the war as a young man of 19. **malison** – curse. **gouts** – drops, meaning bullets.

p.43 THIEPVAL WOOD
Written 1916, published 1930. Published in *Poems 1914-30*. *CP*: "At that moment, north of the Ancre was comparatively calm. One watched the great commotion on the south side." The setting is described in *UW*. EB is delivering heavy materials for the dump in Hamel in the Ancre Valley. As he walked down the hill he looked towards Thiepval Wood which 'leapt alive with tossing flares, which made it seem a monstrous height, and with echo after echo in stammering mad pursuit the guns threshed that area:' (*UW*, p.94)

p.44 BLEUE MAISON
Written June 1917, published 1930. Published in *Poems 1914-30*. Another early war poem in which EB uses landscape to describe another face to war. *CP* "Again, not far west of Saint Omer. There is a place called something like Bleue Maison, but I fancy I have got it a bit out of order. What beautiful moments of just seeing what the world was like, while awaiting what, God knows what." He wrote in his book *The Mind's Eye* (Jonathan Cape, 1934): "War is not all war and there lies the heart of the monster." **St. Elmo's fire** – electric light seen playing about a ship's mast in stormy weather. **Odysseys** – a reminder that war is omnipresent; Odysseus fought in the Trojan War and the Odyssey describes his ten year wanderings home from it.

p.45 CLARE'S GHOST
Written 1917, published 1920. Published in *The Waggoner*. Another poem which survived the uncertain conditions of the trenches. The book of John Clare's poetry which he carried in the trenches, disappeared when his friend Edmund Kapp went off with it (*UW*, p.40.) *CP*: "Written in war surroundings, from Framfield memories." Framfield is in Sussex where the Blunden family lived for a while when EB was at Christ's Hospital, where he came across John Clare in A. Symons'

edition. He dedicated *Three Poems* (1916) to Clare with the words: "Truly he caught the soul of the village and farm in the fine-meshed net of poetry surprisingly beautiful." EB and Alan Porter unearthed much forgotten Clare material and published *John Clare: Poems Chiefly from Manuscript* (Cobden-Sanderson, 1920) which featured 90 poems seen for the first time. **delta of cypress** – group of cypress trees. The branches of these trees carried at funerals were symbols of death. **glebe gate** – church gate.

p.46 REUNION IN WAR
Published 1920. First published in *The Nation*, 20 November 1920; reprinted in *The Shepherd*. Written in the style of a romantic ballad. The night time visit to his lover is also reminiscent of some narrative verse settings. Blunden wrote of narrative poetry:

> 'It is romance in closest relation to the ways of existence, and asking no strange, sudden transcendings of the imagination. The lyric and the ballad...require of us an immediate sublimity of our own.' (Introduction to *A Book of Narrative Verse*, Collins, 1930).

Here Blunden brings the ballad right into the 20th century, combining the past with the present with references to his World War experience. **glebe** – the land attached to the parish church, here meaning the path to the churchyard. **strook** – archaic use of the past tense of the verb to strike. **bullace** – shrub in the same family as the sloe. **cereclothed** – a cerecloth is a winding sheet for corpses.

p.48 1916 SEEN FROM 1921
Published 1920. First published December 1920 in *The New Keepsake for the Year 1921* (The Chelsea Bookclub, 1920 pp.55-56); reprinted in *The Shepherd*. This poem was initially titled: *Festubert 1916*. EB draws the same landscape in *UW*, when he writes: "Acres of self sown wheat glistened and sighed as we wound our way between....the lizard ran warless in the warm dust " (p.37). **redoubt** – a fortification.

p.49 A FARM NEAR ZILLEBEKE

Published 1922. First published in *The Shepherd*. *CP*: "Early 1917, farm near 'Vince Street', it had not long to wait." **hame** – one of the two curved bars of a draught-horse's collar. This poem touches on one of EB's main themes in his war poetry, man's capacity to destroy not just himself but his environment as well.

p.50 BEHIND THE LINE

Published 1922. First published in *The Shepherd*. *CP*: "Some of us were driven back by the world of peace and its puzzles to the company of the years of terror." **pyramid-fosse** – as EB is looking across the landscape he sees the pyramid-like banks of the trenches.

p.51 THIRD YPRES, A REMINISCENCE

Published 1922. First published in *The Shepherd*. This poem describes the involvement of EB's battalion in the Third Battle of Ypres begun on 31 July 1917 and finished at midnight on 2 August 1917. There is a prose account of this same event in *UW* p197. **fascined** – filled with brushwood. **unplashed** – unwoven. **lyddite** – explosive.

p.55 RURAL ECONOMY (1917)

Published 1922. First published in *The Nation and The Athenaeum* 1922, and then in *To Nature*. Here Blunden's use of metaphor and irony come together to present a living picture of how the Generals were farming war. Although Blunden was not known, as Sassoon was, for being critical of the war, this poem strongly demonstrates his attitude to the military planners' abuse of young men's lives. *AH* "Observatory Ridge, looking back towards Scherpenberg." **Thule** – meaning extreme. Thule was an island far north of Orkney discovered by Pytheas (4th century BC). It has been variously identified as Iceland, Shetland, Norway.

p.56 TWO VOICES

Published 1924. First published in *Weekly Westminster* 1924 and then in *Masks of Time*. EB gives the place for this poem as

Hinges near Lacouture. *CP*: " He: Capt. Wallace, our Adjutant. 'King Edward's Road'? Before the march to the Somme." *UW* (p 38).

p.57 THE ZONNEBEKE ROAD
Published 1925. First published in *Masks of Time*. *CP*: "Hard weather: Potijze trenches, and they were poor." Haymarket – a communication trench near Potijze in the Ypres Salient, for walking cases only following a raid.

p.58 PILLBOX
Published 1925. First published in *Masks of Time*. AH: "Sept. 29, 1917. Tower Hamlets, Menin Rd." Tower Hamlets was a battle position on the Menin Road, in the Ypres Salient. Worley – Corporal Frank Worley, one of EB's closest companions in the war. A butcher in Worthing, Sussex, before the war, he was an expert at putting up barbed wire and he and EB often worked together doing this. EB wrote of him in *UW* (p.66): "A kinder heart there never was; a gentler spirit never." Charon – in Greek mythology the ferryman who rowed the dead across the river Styx in the underworld.

p.59 THE PROPHET
Published: 1925. First published in *Masks of Time*. *CP*: "Written after the war, but as from 1917." Waterloo – near Brussels, where Napoleon was finally defeated by the British in 1815. mixen – dunghill. blood-leat – a leat is a trench for bringing water to a mill wheel. Cassandra – a daughter of Priam, King of Troy, who was given the gift of prophecy but not of being believed.

p.61 VLAMERTINGHE: PASSING THE CHATEAU, JULY 1917
Published 1928. Published in *UW*. *CP*: "It was still a fine-looking Chateau, with a 12 inch battery close to the front view." First line is a quotation from John Keats' *Ode on a Grecian Urn* (verse 4).

p.62 CONCERT PARTY: BUSSEBOOM
Published 1928. Published in *UW*. *CP*. "This was as it actually

happened, on an early spring evening in 1917, — the 47th Division I think gave the Revue, in a large hut not far from Vlamertinghe." In a BBC radio interview with James Reeves in 1966, EB explained that although this poem was written years later it "was actually composed in my mind almost at the moment we came out of our own concert". **Larch Wood** – this was a famous British tunnel system. The British miners in the tunnels were confronted when the Germans got in. They had only their fists and feet to defend themselves.

p.63 ANOTHER JOURNEY FROM BETHUNE TO CUINCHY
Published 1928. Published in *UW*. "Imaginary dialogue between EB 1916 and EB 1924 or later." *AH*. **Kingsclere** – a front line sector between Bethune and Cuinchy. **darnel** – rye grass. **red-hatted cranks** – Military Police were distinguished by an arm band and a red cap cover hence their nickname Red Caps. **lime juice** – the soldiers were given lime juice to keep scurvy at bay. **dagged** – bedraggled. **Coldstream Lane** – another part of the trench system.

p.67 AN INFANTRYMAN
Published May 1928. Published in *English Review*, (May 1928, Vol. 46, p.599); then in *Retreat* 1928. "Having nothing much to do one afternoon near Mailly (I think) James Cassels and I went for a long walk in the rain. The poem is on him." EB made many friends during the war, Cassels was one. There is a photo of Cassels in: *Edmund Blunden (On the Trail of the Poets of the Great War)* by Helen McPhail and Phillip Guest (Leo Cooper, Pen and Sword Books, 1999). "Wherever you went, you saw a friend; if you drifted into the quartermaster's stores out of the line, there was this lively pleasure of welcome and acceptance; if you called to the snipers in their lair in the saphead, there would be a cheerful response, the sackcloth that hung behind them and their soon closed loophole would soon be drawn aside to admit you, and you sat with them and their telescope in the knowledge that they were glad. Every face and every name was intensely known to you, while that life lasted." (*Fall in Ghosts*, by Edmund Blunden, The White Owl Press, 1932, p.13).

p.68 PREMATURE REJOICING

Published 1930. Published in *Poems 1914-30*. *CP* "Illustrates my meeting with Realists in August 1916." **Titania** – the queen of fairyland, wife of Oberon, in Shakespeare's *Midsummer Night's Dream*.

p.69 INTO THE SALIENT

Published 1930. Published in *Poems 1914-1930*. *CP* "We went north into the Ypres salient and town, and it was a little time before we knew how overlooked by the German positions every place was." **estaminet** – a small bar/café. **Poperinghe** – small town near Ypres.

p.70 THE MEMORIAL, 1914-1918

Published 1931. Published in *New English Poems* – collected by Lascelles Abercrombie (Victor Gollancz Ltd, 1931); then published in *Halfway House*. **The Memorial** – the Thiepval Memorial designed by Sir Edwin Lutyens. Mentioned in Sylva Norman and EB's *We'll Shift Our Ground* (Cobden Sanderson, 1933, p.178).

p.71 NOVEMBER 1, 1931

Published 1932. Published in *Halfway House* (Cobden-Sanderson, 1932). This poem is a good example of EB's war hauntedness. **November 1, 1931** – EB's 35th birthday. **Menin Gate** – at the start of the route out of Ypres towards the front line, along the Menin Road. There was at that time simply a gap in the ramparts. The original gate had been demolished long before the war to widen the road. **sublunar** – earthly. **sweet red-smiling love** – the love of his dead fellow soldiers.

p.72 THE LOST BATTALION

Published 1934. Published in *Choice or Chance*. Several of Blunden's poems have a nightmarish quality about them. He dreamt about the war most nights.

p.73 AT RUGMER

Published 1934. Published in *Choice or Chance*. **Rugmer** – a hill near Yalding in Kent. **kex** – dried up plant stem. **sere** – dry.

p.74 TO WILFRED OWEN
Published February 1940. Published in *The Cherwell* (February 1940, Vol. 58, No.3, p.42); then published in *Augury — An Oxford Miscellany of Verse and Prose* (edited by Alec M. Hardie and Keith C. Douglas, Basil Blackwell, 1940). EB was the first person to edit Owen's poems. See *The Poems of Wilfred Owen* (Chatto and Windus, 1931).

p.75 BY THE BELGIAN FRONTIER
Published December 1939/January 1940. Published in *Kingdom Come* (Dec/Jan 1939/1940, Vol.1, No.2, p.41); then published in *Fear No More* (Cambridge University Press, 1940); then in *Poems 1930-40* (Macmillan & Co Ltd, 1940). browsing-bell – probably the bell worn by cattle or sheep. the twentieth year – since the Great War.

p.76 SICK BED
Written in 1919, published August 1920. Published in *The Waggoner*. EB's first daughter, Joy, was born in July 1919; on 27 August she died, aged 5 weeks, apparently from contaminated milk. "This was a grief beyond anything I had felt in the War. It has never been quite overcome." (undated draft in possession of the Blunden Estate). twelves – a set of twelve books. rathe-ripe – rathe means eager, early or quick, possibly here he means young or early ripened round cheeks. grutching – grudging. hedge – gather round.

p.78 THE CHILD'S GRAVE
Published 1922. Published in *The Shepherd*. Another Joy poem. She was buried in the churchyard at Kirtling, just outside Cheveley, Suffolk. The grave is unmarked. EB and Mary were living with her family at Deve Cottage nearby. stocks – flowers. coppice and ley – small wood and pathways.

p.80 TO JOY
Published 1923. Published in *To Nature* (printed by The Beaumont Press, June 1923). The composer Gerald Finzi set this poem to music. EB did give his own blood to his daughter, in a last effort to save Joy's life, with a transfusion.

p.81 A "FIRST IMPRESSION" (TOKYO)

Published October 1924. First published in *The London Mercury*, October 1924, frequently published thereafter and appearing in *The Augustan Books of Modern Poetry* (Ernest Benn Ltd., 1925); and then in *A Japanese Garland* (The Beaumont Press, 1928). Another Joy poem; the dead baby refers to her. EB went to Japan in 1924 to take up the post of Professor of English at the Imperial University of Tokyo. He was 27 years old. Mary and their two children, Clare and John stayed behind in Suffolk. **Orcus** – the abode of the dead. **two younglings** – Clare and John.

p.83 A DREAM

Published 1925. Published in *Masks of Time*. **Pactolus** – After Midas, King of Phrygia, asked the gods that everything he touched be turned to gold, his food became gold. He then prayed for this request to be undone. The gods ordered him to bathe in the river Pactolus and after that the river always flowed over golden sands. **gold sands amorous** – In *CP* EB has crossed out these words and written in the margin: "golden sands turned lover". **perdu** – the fish, which is in a hopeless position. EB was a keen angler as a boy and he often writes about fish in his poetry.

p.85 THE ESCAPE

Published 1928. Published in *Retreat*. EB's interest in 'things quiet and unconcerned', (a phrase from his poem "Seers" in *A Hong Kong House*, Collins, 1962) is evident in this poem.

p.86 VALUES

Published 1929. First published in *The Observer*, June 1929 and then *Near and Far* (Cobden-Sanderson 1929). This sonnet was read at EB's funeral in January 1974. **belfried cities** – towns such as Ypres in Belgium.

p.87 THE KISS

Published 1931. First published in *The New Statesman & Nation*, (28 February 1931, p.17) *To Themis* (The Beaumont Press, 1931). **kobold** – a spirit of the mines (in German folklore). **aconite** – a yellow, early flowering spring plant.

p.89 ANOTHER ALTAR
Published 1932. First published in *Queen's Quarterly*, (August 1932, Vol. 39, No.3, pp. 423-424) and then in *Halfway House* (Cobden-Sanderson, 1932). **Tanagra** – a town in ancient Greece. **droughty** – parched.

p.91 MENTAL HOSPITAL, II: POOR TOM'S WELCOME
Published 1932. Published in *Halfway House*. EB was no stranger to mental asylums. His own maternal grandmother, on losing her husband early, was admitted to Barming asylum where he visited her as a child. Throughout his life he displayed an interest in writers who struggled with mental difficulties. On the title-page of his copy of his own edition of *Poems by Ivor Gurney* (Hutchinson,1954) which is in possession of the Estate of Mrs Claire Blunden, he has written: "It seems my destiny to edit Poets whose minds gave way!
    John Clare
    Christopher Smart
    William Collins
And now poor old Ivor Gurney, the only one I saw in real life. 'And I see him yet' and hear him too – singing and playing to 'a naked frosty sky'." EB visited Gurney at the asylum in Dartford. **raree-show** – spectacle.

p.92 A TALE NOT IN CHAUCER
Published 1932. First published in *Queen's Quarterly*, (February 1932, Vol. 39, No.1, pp. 81-82) and then in *Halfway House*. An example of EB's lighter, witty and gently ironic side.

p.94 MINORITY REPORT
Published 1937. Published in *An Elegy and Other Poems* (Cobden-Sanderson, 1937). **Horatius** – the Latin lyric poet and satirist (65-8 BC). **van** – form of vanguard.

p.95 WRITING A SKETCH OF A FORGOTTEN POET
Published 1937. Published in *An Elegy and Other Poems*. In his Preface to *Poems 1930-1940* (Macmillan, 1940) he writes: "The name of the forgotten poet at page 145 was Mary Leapor, a most attractive young writer of the eighteenth century, and regarded as a prodigy because she was also the daughter of a gardener."

p.96 CHAFFINCH ON SUBURBAN GROWTHS
Published 1937. Published in *An Elegy and Other Poems*.

P.97 THE KIND STAR
Published April 1939. First published in *On Several Occasions, By a Fellow of Merton College*, (April 1939); then in *Poems 1930-40*.

p.98 THE SUM OF ALL
Published 1939. First published in *The Listener*, (16 March 1939, p. 572) and then in *Poems 1930-40*. prolepsis – anticipation.

p.99 GOD'S TIME
Written 19 December 1943, published 1943. First published in the *Times Literary Supplement*, 25 December 1943, p.618, and then in *Shells by a Stream* (Macmillan & Co., 1944). windflowers – wood anemones.

p.100 HIGH ELMS, BRACKNELL
Published 1949. Published in *After the Bombing*. Claire and EB visited High Elms House in Bracknell (near Windsor) where the poet Shelley lived with his wife Harriet and their baby Ianthe in 1813, while EB was writing his biography of Shelley (published in 1946). Two buds – these were poppies which Claire pressed in her copy of *Shelley* and which are still in existence. incubus – an oppressive influence. Harriet – Shelley's young wife; she married the 19 year old Shelley at 16 and their marriage did not last.

p.101 DOG ON WHEELS
Published 1962. Published in *A Hong Kong House* (Collins, 1962). In 1953 EB took the position of Professor of English at Hong Kong University. The stuffed woolly dog on wheels belonged to his youngest daughter. Being in Hong Kong was not necessarily an easy time for Blunden. He was a long way from all that he loved in England, and at times he felt isolated. This poem is imbued with sadness and a sense of isolation.

p.102 EASTERN TEMPEST
Published 1927. Published in *Study of English*, (June 1927, No.3, pp. 236-237); then in *Japanese Garland*.

p.103 A JAPANESE EVENING
Published 1930. Published in *Poems 1914-30*.

p.105 AFTER THE BOMBING
Published 1949. Published in *After the Bombing* In 1947 EB was invited by the Foreign Office to go to Japan, after World War II, as a cultural advisor as part of the work of reconciliation. EB believed strongly in the idea that literature rather than politics could help to heal the wounds of war. He stayed until May 1950.

p.106 AN ISLAND TRAGEDY
Published 1962. Published in *A Hong Kong House*. our hill – EB's house (which has since been pulled down) in Hong Kong stood on a hillside within the University compound. From the house he could look up to the top of the hill as well as down to the harbour below. EB's poetic imagination was peopled with symbolic gods. Here the wood god (nature) is threatened by the increasing urban sprawl of Hong Kong.

p.107 A HONG KONG HOUSE
Published 1955. First published in *The Quill* (1955, Vol.1, p.21), and also (in holograph form) by the Poetry Book Society Limited, 1959, and then in *A Hong Kong House*. The poem was written while EB was Professor of English at Hong Kong University. The garden was overlooked by a long veranda

which ran the length of the side of EB's house. It was an informal garden, dominated by a soaring palm tree, which looked down to the university buildings and the sea beyond. For an analysis of this poem, there is an article by Prof. J. Preston entitled *A Language not our Own: The Language of Literature* (University of Hong Kong Supplement to the Gazette, Vol XXXII, 14 June 1985). The poem, as presented here, follows the holograph version. **holm-like** – a tree reminding him of an evergreen oak, similar to holly. **playthings** – refers to his daughters' toys left on the lawn.

p.108 A SWAN, A MAN
Written 1964, published March 1966. Published in *Eleven Poems* (The Golden Head Press, Cambridge, 1966). The setting is the old mill pool next to Hall Mill (in Long Melford, Suffolk), the house where EB retired, in 1964, after his post in Hong Kong. **Ancient Mariner** – the cursed, central figure in Coleridge's poem. EB was still, at the age of 68, suffering from survivor guilt and memories of the war.

p.109 ANCRE SUNSHINE
Written 3 September 1966, published 1968. Published in *Garland* (The Golden Head Press, Cambridge, 1968). The setting for this poem is the Ancre Valley. EB made several visits to the battlefields and this was probably written during his last visit. It was his final poem and has the distinction of being the last poem about the war published by any surviving soldier poet. **Miraumont** – a village just north of Grandcourt. It was taken from the Germans by the British in February 1917. **Arras** – the centre of heavy conflict in 1914 and 1917. **the mill** – there is reference to this mill in one of EB's earlier poems about the Ancre entitled: "The Ancre at Hamel: Afterwards", published 1924:

> I heard it crying, that sad rill,
>   Below the painful ridge,
> By the burnt unraftered mill
>   And the relic of a bridge.

His use of time, moving backwards and forwards, linking his present and past, is the mechanism which underpins EB's final comment on the war. Claire was 23 years younger than him and represents a later generation for Blunden. The first two verses describe peaceful moments in the present before memories of the war intervene. She then appears to be distanced and, as he imagines her standing by the now vanished mill, witnessing how it looked in 1917, the present merges with the past. In his poetic imagination, EB, via Claire, takes us back again into the world of war. In the last two lines he gives us a glimpse of a continuing reality in the then and there, together with the continuing reality of his here and now, leaving us with the question of whether anything is ever finally over.

p.110 THE WATCHERS
Published 1927. First published in *St Martin's Review*, (November 1927, No. 441, p.568) and then in *UW*. EB is thinking of his own death. This poem seems appropriate as a final word from EB for whom the love of his fellow soldier was so significant.